The Ultimate Wood Pellet Grill Smoker Cookbook

THE ULTIMATE
Wood Pellet Grill
SMOKER COOKBOOK

100+ Recipes
for Perfect Smoking

BILL WEST

Photography by Marija Vidal

ROCKRIDGE
PRESS

For general information on our other products and services or to obtain technical support, please contact our Customer Care Department within the United States at (866) 744-2665, or outside the United States at (510) 253-0500.

Rockridge Press publishes its books in a variety of electronic and print formats. Some content that appears in print may not be available in electronic books, and vice versa.

TRADEMARKS: Rockridge Press and the Rockridge Press logo are trademarks or registered trademarks of Callisto Media Inc. and/or its affiliates, in the United States and other countries, and may not be used without written permission. All other trademarks are the property of their respective owners. Rockridge Press is not associated with any product or vendor mentioned in this book.

Interior Designers: Liz Cosgrove and Katy Brown
Cover Designers: Alyssa Nassner and Amy King
Photo Art Director: Karen Beard
Editor: Salwa Jabado
Production Editor: Andrew Yackira

Photography by Marija Vidal, © 2018; food styling by Cregg Green. Author photo courtesy Kristin Lee, Lucky 13 Photography.

Illustrations: page 6, by Paul Girard, © 2018; page 8 © IntergalacticDesignStudio/iStock.com; page 21 © Forest Foxy/Shutterstock.com.

ISBN: Print 978-1-64152-217-5
eBook 978-1-64152-218-2

To the foodies, friends,
and readers who have been
following the smoke signals at
my site, BarbecueTricks.com.
Thanks for sharing.

CONTENTS

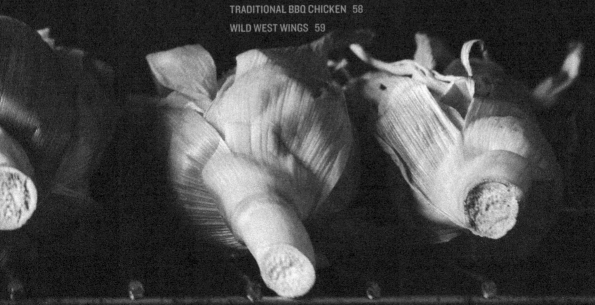

INTRODUCTION

In the spring of 2009 I went to my first barbecue school. It was a three-day course that unveiled all the word-of-mouth secrets that pit masters don't like to put in writing. After all, competition teams like their secrets, but they also like to share with friends. This is where I first learned many of the tips, tricks, and basics of competition versus backyard cooking.

I'll never forget seeing the little jet engine with a thermostat called a wood pellet cooker. The compact fire pot inside was burning so hot I had to film an inside-look video. The big selling point at the time was that this seemingly magic plug-in machine was compliant with stringent barbecue competition sanctioning rules. It truly uses wood for the heat source. Electricity powers the small fan, but that's it. It was hard to believe the amount of intense fire that little bit of wood created. The sound of its tiny jet engine amazed me, too.

In my first book, *BBQ Blueprint*, I talk about some of the hassles you deal with for competition cooking versus regular backyard cooking. To me, the challenges you have to wrestle with to optimize one single-judged bite aren't what I love about the barbecue . . . but the wood pellet grill smoker can really do it all. This is just the kind of trickery I love! With the pellet grill, you get competition quality with a simplicity that aligns with my laid-back "set-it-and-forget-it" lifestyle.

In short, I love a low, slow cook. To many, that's the true definition of "barbecue": low-and-slow in lieu of hot-and-fast. That's why a good portion of the recipes in this book really take advantage of the low, steady smoking temperatures despite the fact that today's wood pellet grills have the unique ability to maintain hot and fast temperatures over 400°F.

In this book, you'll get a concise overview of how to easily harness the special powers of a wood pellet grill and smoker. Yes, it is truly a grill *and* smoker all in one. It offers precise control to slow smoke a brisket for hours, as well as higher-temperature grilling to prep perfect and quick pork chops (something a typical smoker doesn't get hot enough to handle).

◀ **PIG POPS,** page 69

I have also included loads of recipes that work great on a wood pellet grill. There are plenty of recipes here for traditional barbecue, like low-and-slow ribs, brisket, and pulled pork roast. I go back to these recipes time and time again. Plus, I have added a bunch of recipes that take advantage of the grill's high-heat settings—fun stuff like smoked, or "smo-fried," chicken, and even desserts.

My blog is called Barbecue Tricks because I love finding hacks for better barbecue, and I've always thought that the way the wood pellet grill works really is a trick in and of itself. It's a tiny yet raging campfire in an easy-to-handle outdoor oven.

It uses real wood! It's as simple as an electric grill! It's almost too easy.

Pro tip: If you want a bit more "me time" with your grill, you don't have to let your spouse know how easy it is. Just grab a good lawn chair and your favorite book, and let the family know you're tending the fire. It's not a lie.

A few years into smoking with my Traeger Texas Elite pellet grill as well as several gas, charcoal, and electric smokers later, I can confirm that pellet power is my favorite way to go. It's easier than chopping logs and fighting flames, it's cleaner than messy charcoal, and it's just as fast to start as gas, with much better flavor.

Let's get smokin'.

Part One

THE FUNDAMENTALS OF WOOD PELLET SMOKING

Chapter 1
GOING
WOOD PELLET

Real barbecue can be hard; you've got hot embers, dirty coals, dangerous fire, plus a lot of TLC and time to invest. But the results are the reward for the hard work. Succulent and savory smoke-infused dishes just can't be achieved without low temperatures, a bit of time, and quality hardwood smoke. Charcoal briquettes are okay, but they're messy. Hardwood logs are great for barbecue purists, but massive log-burning grills are overkill for most patios. Wood pellet fuel has made barbecue a lot easier. The tiny pellets burn just like logs, but leave very little ash and are easy to manage.

Today's wood pellet grills offer all the convenience of electric smokers with a few added benefits, including higher temperature options; real wood-generated cooking heat; and no soot or wasted fuel, because the pellets are devoid of any of the moisture you would get from green or wet wood. ◊

WHY WE'RE PELLET HEADS

First, a little history. Smoke has been used throughout the ages for preserving meats. In fact, the process of smoking and curing meats evolved over the centuries to prevent disease and increase food safety. The advent of modern food preservation methods means that around the world today, curing meats is more about cultural value, taste, and texture than it is about food safety. In some underdeveloped countries, however, curing is still a viable means of making sure meat remains safe during production and transportation.

Following a cure, meats have been traditionally "smoked." Smoking typically involves hanging salted meats in a dedicated smokehouse and letting them soak up smoke from low-heat smoldering fires. The process adds flavor and color to the meat and inhibits rancidity. Most of us smoke and cure because we love the taste and texture it gives to food, but it is good to be aware of food safety when dealing with raw meats.

Wood pellet grills are just the latest step in the long tradition of smoking as the selection of commercially available smokers continues to grow. First, the Weber company introduced and popularized the charcoal kettle grill back in the '50s and later introduced the still-beloved Smokey Mountain Cooker that specialized in smoking with charcoal. Later, offset "stick burners" became popular as the competition barbecue world blossomed. A stick burner uses split logs, or hardwood "sticks," to generate smoke in a fire box adjacent to the cook chamber. Using indirect heat and smoke flow is how the pros like to cook . . . often in massive trailer-pulled black steel smokers. In the '80s, Joe Traeger developed and patented the pellet cooker process. To this day, the Traeger name is almost synonymous with wood pellet grills. (More on Joe in a bit.)

There is a lot to love about wood pellet grills, and a few things of which you need to be aware. The pellet grill requires electricity, so you'll need access to power when cooking. That's something to plan for, both in camping and competition situations. Also, some cooks find the price of wood pellets unacceptable. And if you are a charcoal flavor purist, you likely will not be satisfied with the flavor that results from cooking with pellets.

But there are many reasons to *love* wood pellet grills:

★ You are cooking with clean hardwood. This is true smoke flavor in its purest form.

★ If you're looking to cook with a wood pellet grill in competitions, it's approved for that use.

★ The "set-it-and-forget-it" simplicity makes the wood pellet grill as easy to use as your home oven. These cookers are built to sustain low and steady temperatures without needing a lot of tending.

★ It is the cleanest way to get wood flavor: no messy charcoal or stoking wood into fire boxes. The wood is in tidy and transportable pellet form.

★ The wood pellet grill smoker can run unattended for hours on end—eight hours without reloading is common, depending on the size of the hopper (the part of the grill that stores and feeds the pellets into the grill).

★ The newest wood pellet grill smokers are coveted for their ability to dial up higher temperatures for searing, roasting, and outdoor baking.

A BRIEF HISTORY OF WOOD PELLET GRILLS

Wood pellet grills grew out of the wood pellet home heating industry that blossomed during the 1970s oil crisis. Wood pellet home heaters became increasingly popular due to the rising price of oil.

Joe Traeger, whose family operated an Oregon heating company, took the wood pellet concept to the grill and patented the first wood pellet grill smoker in 1986. His simple original design had the look of a traditional offset smoker, and the electronics and thermostat features continued to develop over the years.

Thanks to that patent, Traeger was the only manufacturer in town for 20 years. Then, when the patent expired, other companies started to produce wood pellet grills. Joe sold off Traeger after the expiration of his patent, but the company that bears his name remains the big dog in the wood pellet grill world.

By 2008, there were a handful of newcomers to the industry, and the pellet story continued to grow. By 2014, there were 27 manufacturers on record. More companies are getting in on the action every year. Some new models feature stainless-steel accents, higher-heat searing, and wireless Bluetooth controls.

THE INS AND OUTS OF A WOOD PELLET GRILL SMOKER

The inner workings of a wood pellet grill are simple yet impressive. The fuel is 100 percent hardwood with no fillers. No petroleum products are added, just the compressed hardwood pellets that resemble rabbit chow. And before you ask, no, you don't want to try to smoke rabbit chow. You would think that a little wood pellet would burn with a soft flame like a candle. Surprisingly, just a few pellets dropped into a teacup-size fire pot can create a large jet of clean heat when stoked by a thermostat-controlled fan. The sight and sound are amazing.

To the eye, a typical wood pellet grill looks straightforward. It's a barrel-shaped grill with an electric thermostat attached to a thermometer inside the cooking chamber. Hidden beneath the grate and a large drip plate is the fire pot, where the real magic happens.

★ The **hopper** is a covered box that holds your pellets. Hoppers range in size to hold 10 to 40 pounds of pellets, and are typically positioned as a side box. Some newer models position the hopper along the entire back length of the wood pellet grill. Look for features like an easy clean-out door, a window to gauge remaining fuel, and a cover to prevent moisture. Note: Wet pellets are useless.

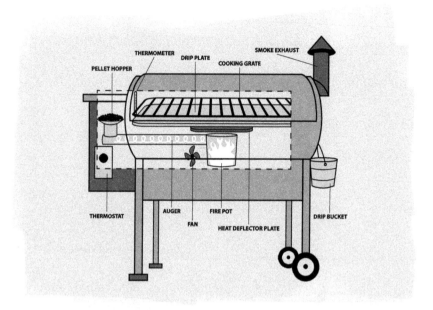

* The **auger** is a helical-shaped mechanism that slowly transports a small, slow, and steady flow of pellets through a tube to the fire pot. The flow speed is controlled by the thermostat.

* The **fire pot** is typically positioned in the center bottom area of the smoker. The pellets are ignited and stoked into a small but raging furnace by a small fan. Surprisingly little ash accumulates in the fire pot. Ashes eventually accumulate around the bottom of this cup, and occasional clean-out is necessary. Because the fire pot takes the most abuse of the entire grill, look for ones made of durable, high-quality steel, or stainless steel.

* The **heat deflector** is a heavy steel plate that covers the direct heat of the fire pot and disperses the heat like a convection oven. A large drip plate, placed above the deflector plate, drains all the drippings away from any open flame so there are no grease fires or flareups.

TOP BRANDS AND WHAT THEY DO BEST

Wood pellet grills are enjoying a surge in popularity these days. This means there are new companies jumping into the arena and that established players are continuing to expand their product lines. Here are a few of the top brands and their hallmarks.

TRAEGER

Joe Traeger's namesake brand of wood pellet grill smokers remains tops in the business. These days, the company is growing, employing about 130 people, and its headquarters have moved from Oregon to Utah. Traeger has the benefit of being the original, with lots of hard-earned experience in the wood pellet grill niche. You'll find plenty of experienced Traeger fans and critics trying to grab Traeger's market share.

Traeger grill prices vary, with the most popular model going for just under $999 and other smaller units under $500. Traegers are well-built, shaped like a horizontal barrel smoker with a distinct smokestack and a signature tin drip bucket. Size of the unit is the main factor in pricing.

REC TEC

Rec Tec is a newer company that touts quality and value; its grills include a larger hopper to hold 40 pounds of pellets for longer cooks. The hopper will continue to feed the fire as needed and is positioned along the back of the cook chamber, allowing for a shorter auger. Rec Tec is also known for its liberal use of high-grade 304 stainless steel in the cooking grate, fire pot, and signature bull's-horn handles. The six-year warranty is also notable for being much longer than that of other manufacturers.

Rec Tec prices are typically a bit lower by model than the comparable Traeger models. The most popular model, the Stampede, is priced at $899. But at $399, the new low-cost Bullseye model gives you a more affordable way to get into wood pellet cooking.

CAMP CHEF

Camp Chef is a company that made its mark in grilling before the pellet cooker revolution. Based out of Cache Valley, Utah, the company sells camp ovens, griddles, and now a line of pellet grills under the name Woodwind. The Woodwind line looks jarringly similar to the Traeger Texas line and boasts high temperatures of up to 500°F. The patented ash clean-out system is also unique, plus it features a cast iron grate and a side sear box. The signature Woodwind model sells for $899.

PIT BOSS

Through Walmart, Pit Boss has introduced the masses to a low-cost wood pellet grill. The Pit Boss story is all about price per square inch of cooking space. The Classic model costs a surprising $396 and features 700 square inches of cook space. Pit Boss grills also feature a flame-broiling option with a slider to expose the fire pot. And their hopper is the only one with a convenient small window to let you gauge remaining pellets at a glance without opening. The Pit Boss Classic does not feature the high-quality stainless steel of the other brands listed. You will want to use extra care with the porcelain-coated grate, and the exposed steel may be prone to corrosion.

OTHER BRANDS

There truly has been a surge in new brands of pellet grills over the last few years. Other popular brands include Green Mountain Grills, Z Grills, Fast Eddy's by Cookshack, Grilla Grills, and MAK Grills. No doubt there will be new brands on the scene in the future. Most are manufactured in China (the MAK brand is an American-manufactured exception). The good news is that the primary features of these cookers are the same: the ability to use your hardwood of choice and easily control the heat with a simple thermostat. Expect features like searing burners and remote controls to vary and advance. However, all of the recipes in this book will work nicely with any of the brands and models listed. Most of the differences are cosmetic, or in basic build quality, rather than in features.

CHOOSING FEATURES

Many of the new brands of wood pellet grills resemble the original Traeger, but there are a few features worth noting under the hood. Higher cooking temperatures can allow for faster searing of steaks, stainless steel holds up best to corrosion, and hopper capacity can allow for longer cook times between refills. Most brands now offer remote control options if desired.

MAIN FEATURES OF BEST-SELLING WOOD PELLET GRILL SMOKERS

	TRAEGER PRO SERIES 34	TRAEGER TAILGATER 20	REC TEC 680	REC TEC BULLSEYE	CAMP CHEF WOODWIND PG24WWSS	PIT BOSS CLASSIC (WALMART)	GREEN MOUNTAIN DANIEL BOONE
GRATE	Porcelain-coated steel	Porcelain-coated steel	Stainless steel	Porcelain-coated steel	Cast iron	Porcelain-coated cast iron	Stainless steel
COOKING AREA	884 sq. in.	300 sq. in.	702 sq. in.	380 sq. in.	570 sq. in.	700 sq. in.	458 sq. in.
TEMPERATURE RANGE	150°F to 450°F	150°F to 400°F	180°F to 500°F+	200°F to 550°F	160°F to 500°F	180°F to 500°F+	150°F to 500°F
COLOR/FINISH	Powder-coated steel; available in bronze and blue	Powder-coated steel; available in bronze and blue	High-temp powder-coated steel	Baked-on porcelain enamel	Steel	High-temp black powder-coated steel; available in bronze look	Optional stainless-steel door
PRICE	$999	$449	$998	$399	$899	$396	$599
MANUFACTURED	China	China	China	China	China	China	China
WARRANTY	3 years	3 years	6 years	1 year	3 years	1 year	2 years
HOPPER CAPACITY	18 lbs.	8 lbs.	40 lbs.	15 lbs.	18 lbs.	21 lbs.	17 lbs.
SIDE OR SEARING BURNER	No	No	No	No	Yes	Yes	No

KNOW YOUR SMOKER

As the pit master, your job is to control the cook. Your life will be made a bit easier with a good pellet smoker, but there are still a few variables to which you'll want to pay close attention.

Time: From preheating to resting the meat after a cook, you'll want to put some extra thought and planning into the amount of time you will need. Most wood pellet grills have an important preheat time frame to observe. When working low and slow with larger cuts of meat, your cook times can be quite long. Start early and give yourself plenty of wiggle room to hit your desired serving time. Even after you pull the meat off the grill, there's an extra 10-minute "rest" recommended for large cuts of meat before carving.

The meat: Your "cooking" experience starts at the butcher shop or grocery with your selection of the best-looking cuts. Quality meats with more fat provide the best flavor. Remember: the bigger the cuts, the more cook time and seasoning you'll need.

Spices: We have great seasoning blends mapped out in the recipes in this book. Freshness makes a difference; use the freshest spices you can get your hands on. You can also "bloom" some spices in a dry frying pan over low heat to activate the oils and enhance flavors.

Smoke type: Choose your wood pellet flavor to match your meat. We'll cover this more in the next chapter, but the wood you choose affects the consistency of these recipes.

Placement: Your wood pellet grill has a very even cooking temperature devoid of typical hot spots, thanks to the convection-like heat circulation caused by the fan and the heat deflector. Still, try to position your food in the pathway of the smoke inside the chamber.

Temperature: Lower cook temperatures for smoking provide the most effective way to break down collagen and fat in the meat and absorb maximum smoke flavor. Outside temperature can also affect cook temperature and time. Try to position your wood pellet grill out of the way of direct harsh winds.

THE LOWDOWN ON TEMPERATURE

On typical grills, I always suggest setting up hot and cold "zones" where you can move meats to control cooking speeds. That tactic is not an option on wood pellet grills. Instead, you'll be working with set levels of heat, such as hot-smoking, cold-smoking, and smoke-roasting. This book focuses on traditional smoking at lower temperatures—most low-and-slow meat smoking takes place between 225°F and 275°F. It's at these lower temperatures that the real magic happens. With this set-it-and-forget-it style of wood pellet cooking, low-temperature meats are gently coaxed into fall-off-the-bone succulence.

Cooking at lower temperatures, however, won't necessarily keep you from going too far and overcooking your food. Different foods have different internal-temperature targets. For example, leaner cuts of meat dry out easily. If you're not careful, you'll end up with jerky!

When you use your wood pellet grill at higher temperatures, it is best described as smoke-roasting. Like on a gas grill, you'll attain high-heat char and browning; unlike on a gas grill, you'll get smoke flavor. Most of the baking and cooking you can do in your home oven can also be done in these types of smokers. The popular wood pellet grill smokers mentioned in this book can all reach highs well over 400°F. Electric smokers are also easy to operate but have a more limited temperature high end of 275°F. They are not nearly as versatile.

The pellet grill's ability to achieve higher temperatures than a typical smoker is a definite plus, so, when we get to the recipes, we'll sneak in a few specialties that take advantage of high heat, like reverse searing (see page 85).

OPTIONAL GEAR

You'll want a few extra tools to enhance your grilling experience. While not necessary, these accessories help ensure properly cooked foods, ease transport to and from your smoker, lend a hand with meal prep and cleanup, and boost your wood pellet rep. I recommend adding at least a few—if not all—to your arsenal.

DRIP PANS AND BUCKET LINERS

Heavy-duty food service foil with an 18-inch width is the common choice to cover the drip pan in your pellet smoker. Recently, some grill manufacturers have started selling drip pan liners as well as disposable inserts to keep your drip bucket clean. It may seem like overprotection, but drippings and grease are exceptionally stubborn and better to throw out than wash down a sink. I recommend Drip EZ brand liners.

THERMOMETERS

Digital meat thermometers are not only a mandatory cooking aid, but they are also a must for food safety. Most wood pellet grill smokers come with an internal thermometer probe, but you'll probably want a more portable handheld digital instant-read thermometer. The internal temperature of your meat should be within the safe range according to the USDA's food-safety standards. Plus, achieving internal temperature targets are key factors in getting your barbecue perfectly cooked. ThermoWorks makes the Thermapen, which is the gold standard waterproof thermometer; it sells for about $90. However, there are more affordable options available, including Bluetooth probes. These sweet devices measure the internal temperature of individual cuts of meat so the chef can ensure that everyone at the table has the perfect steak—made to order. The Tenergy Solis is a popular unit priced under 60 bucks, and gets great reviews.

SMOKER TUBES

Wood pellet grills are unable to sustain smoke production and temperatures under 120°F. If you are looking to do a lot of cold-smoking of cheese or just want to add extra smoke flavor, do what many pit masters do and use a specially made tube filled with pellets. These tubes can burn on top of the grill grate for hours without generating substantial heat. As a result, they can convert your grill into a cold smoker. The most popular brand is A-Maze-N.

GRILL GRATES

Grill grates are metal panels that replace your grill's stock grates. The benefit is that grill grates cook by conduction (contact), convection (hot air), and infrared (radiant heat), resulting in juicier, more evenly cooked food. This can be a nice addition to a pellet grill if you're fast-grilling filets and burgers. Plus, you get better grill marks!

ELECTRIC KNIVES

Electric knives can help you slice meats to your desired thickness. They're essential tools for cutting your brisket razor-thin.

BEAR "CLAWS"

These handheld pronged forks allow you to pull apart whole roasts for such dishes as authentic pulled pork or carnitas.

FROGMATS

These inexpensive, dishwasher-safe, nonstick, heat-resistant mesh grill mats prevent foods from sticking to your grill grates and make cleanup a snap.

PELLET STORAGE BINS

Pellets are sensitive to moisture. Once wet, they expand and become unusable. Look for canisters with tight-fitting lids. Common five-gallon utility buckets work nicely, and Traeger sells lids for the buckets that make storing and pouring pellets easier.

CAST IRON SKILLET

A cast iron skillet comes in handy for moving foods from smoker to stovetop. With the high-heat settings of a wood pellet grill, a preheated pan can also be used to achieve more surface-area sear on thick steaks.

CEDAR OR OTHER HARDWOOD PLANKS

If you're looking to show off a bit, you can use cedar or other hardwood planks both to add flavor to smoked entrées and to make yourself look über-cool serving smoked fish right on a smoking board! This is a unique and traditional presentation for salmon, and the cedar adds a wonderful flavor above and beyond the wood pellet smoke flavor.

SAFETY, TROUBLESHOOTING, AND MAINTENANCE

Wood pellet grills are incredibly convenient. However, it's important to keep in mind that you are still playing with live fire. You'll want to be prepared to deal with accidents and other issues. Each pellet grill smoker's owner's manual has official information on safety, troubleshooting, and maintenance.

If you are a new wood pellet grill owner, the first step in safety is to follow the manufacturer's instructions for initial firing of the grill. This will burn off any manufacturing oils and bits of Styrofoam packaging that may remain on cooking surfaces.

Never use your wood pellet grill in an enclosed area. The dangerous gasses can accumulate quickly. Grilling inside your home is obviously a smoky and bad idea, but also do not grill in enclosed porches and tents, which are less obviously dangerous.

To stay safe (and be able to enjoy your delicious smoker results), keep the following safety tips in mind at all times.

SAFETY 101

★ Have a dedicated fire extinguisher for your grill area (and another for your kitchen).

★ Never attempt to move a hot grill.

★ Follow the manufacturer's standard starting, preheating, and shutdown procedures. These easy steps will allow you to safely prime and ignite and later extinguish and clear your auger and fire pot. The procedures help prevent unsafe accumulation of pellets in the fire pot.

★ The grill will produce airborne hot embers, so keep kids, pets, flammable liquids, and vinyl siding a safe distance away from it for the entire cooking process.

★ Don't smoke with strange wood, particularly pellets that were not produced specifically for cooking. Non-food-safe pellets can be comprised of scrap wood. Construction scrap wood is often treated with toxic chemicals and other undesirable finishes that you wouldn't want to ingest.

★ Wood pellet grill smoker manufacturers don't want you to leave these cookers on for hours fully unattended. They express this in the owner's manual fine print. You'll also notice that in sales photos, they play it safe—the cook is always in eyeshot across the yard, relaxing in a chaise or in the kitchen keeping the cooker in view from the window.

★ Never operate your wood pellet grill in the rain. Remember, your grill relies on electricity to operate, and electric machines should never get wet. Plus, wood pellets are sensitive to moisture and will swell, disintegrate, and make a mess when wet.

★ Unplug your wood pellet grill when not in use, and avoid linking long extension cords. Even though the grill generates its heat with burning wood, you still have possible electricity dangers. Remember, too, that your pellet grill won't operate if you lose power.

Accidents and mistakes happen all the time, but rest assured that your wood pellet grill is constructed with safety in mind and is safer to operate than charcoal and stick-burning smokers. This is because you don't have to manually add wood to hot coals to stoke the fire. With a wood pellet grill, the small fire pot is tucked away inside the grill and stoked automatically thanks to the auger and the thermostat.

TROUBLESHOOTING TIPS

★ Be sure to always use your manufacturer's start-up and shutdown procedures. These important steps ensure that your auger and fire pot do not accumulate fuel.

★ If you feel like your grill is struggling to maintain heat, cold temperatures may be the culprit. Your wood pellet grill's thermostat should compensate and have your auger and fire pot work harder. Windy conditions can be a sneakier problem. When possible, position your grill to avoid direct wind. Specially constructed insulated grill covers are available from manufacturers (like Traeger) to combat exceptionally windy and cold conditions. It may seem odd for a grill to wear a sweater, but the nonflammable material can safely provide needed insulation in windy and extra-cold conditions.

★ Any smoker is susceptible to delayed cook times due to prying eyes. In fact, every time you open the cook chamber to peek, it can add take up to 15 minutes to regain temperatures. A good wood pellet grill's thermostat can combat this better than most other types of smokers, but if you think your cook times are longer than they should be, it's worth evaluating. As the saying goes, "If you're lookin', you ain't cookin'."

★ Occasional ash cleanup is necessary to keep your grill in good operation. Be sure to do your cleaning before operation, or at least 12 hours after any previous ignition.

★ A dependable power source is important. Unlike charcoal and gas grills, wood pellet grills require electricity to stoke wood pellets into the fire pot. A blown fuse or any interruption in power will make your grill inoperable.

MAINTENANCE TIPS

★ Keep it clean. Your wood pellet grill requires little maintenance other than an occasional removal of ash from the fire pot. When fully cool, you can use a shop vac to remove excess ash in and around the fire pot and cook chamber. This is recommended after three to five cooks (or after exceptionally long cooks).

★ Vacuum the areas in and around the hopper occasionally, as they can accumulate sawdust and pellet remnants after use.

★ Clean your grill grate after each use. Porcelain-coated grates should be scrubbed with a nonmetallic brush to protect the porcelain finish.

★ Never use sprays or liquids to clean the interior of your wood pellet grill.

★ Use a cover when the grill is not in use to protect from bleaching sunlight, moisture, and nesting insects.

★ If you are having ignition or temperature problems, visually inspect the fire pot. Over time, the fire pot is the most commonly replaced part on wood pellet grills; due to intense heat and constant use, it is more susceptible to corrosion and wear. You can replace yours with any preferred stainless-steel fire pots.

Chapter 2

ALL ABOUT THE WOOD SMOKE

Will it smoke? Due to mankind's long history of cooking over live fire, there are unlimited combinations of animal, vegetable, and hardwood smoke flavor.

Remember: Wood pellet grills should only be fueled by food-safe pellets. With wood pellets, you can mix and match your smoke profile to achieve unique flavors—something you cannot do easily with other smokers. The pellets are also easy to store and move, due to their compact nature. However, note that wood pellet grills are limited to pellet fuel that is available commercially, which can be somewhat expensive, hard to find locally, and/or limited in variety. But with blossoming competition, the price, availability, and variety of wood pellets are getting better every year. ◊

WOOD PELLETS 101

Wood pellet grills have become popular because they offer a level of consistency that burning natural logs cannot. Competition cooks love to know that their heat will stay consistent over time and that flavor profiles will remain the same week in and week out. The compressed sawdust is free from impurities, so wood pellets burn cleanly and effectively, maintaining optimal temperature control. Most wood pellet grills consume about a half pound of pellets per hour on a low smoke setting. At higher temperatures, near 450°F, you'll burn about 2.3 pounds per hour. Wind, weather conditions, and cold meat in the cook chamber will also affect burn rate.

One of the joys of wood pellet grills is finding the perfect hardwood for your recipe. Consider your locale: Texas cooks use a lot of native mesquite and oak. I live in South Carolina, so pecan is indigenous and popular. Finally, competition cooks like to get elaborate, combining blends of different woods or even cooking with layers of wood flavor at different points in the cook. Feel free to experiment.

FOOD-GRADE WOOD PELLETS

I've searched high and low for online and local sources of wood pellets, looking for the best price. Again, the big issue is that you need to use food-grade pellets. I've been able to find 100 percent oak pellets at tempting prices; however, there is still no guarantee that impure and potentially toxic wood finishes, varnish, or worse haven't been mixed into the scrap wood used to make these cheaper versions. That's the importance of the USDA food-grade label.

Many grill manufacturers have also gotten into providing their own brands of hardwood pellets. It's important to note that you don't need to stick with your grill manufacturer's brand of wood pellet. It's good to shop around for pricing.

More and more often, the big box retailers that sell wood pellet grills are also selling pellet fuel. Avoiding shipping costs can help keep your expenses down. Plus, you can occasionally find the best prices locally. The lowest price I've found is $16.88 for a 40-pound sack of food-grade Pit Boss Competition Blend at Lowe's. Online, you can typically find food-grade pellets priced at about $20 for a 20-pound bag. Shipping costs could affect total price, so it would be smart to seek out online retailers that offer free shipping.

When you find a good value on wood pellets, it makes sense to store away a surplus. Not only are pellets food-safe, but there is also no shelf life to worry about. Simply keep them dry and you can store them for years. I also recommend keeping your pellets in rodent- and insect-proof containers.

WOOD FLAVORS DEFINED

Smoke flavor is an element of a recipe that defies other senses. It's a flavor that connects you subconsciously to a primitive smell of a specific time and place. Like revisiting a great song, reexperiencing a smoke-infused bite can take you back to a special time and place in a way that other senses cannot. Building recipes around hardwood flavors is one of the joys of smoking. Have fun experimenting and exploring! The following chart outlines the types of food-grade wood pellets currently available on the market.

SINGLE-FLAVOR FOOD-GRADE WOOD PELLETS

WOOD	FLAVOR	WHAT TO COOK WITH IT
ALDER	Delicate, with a hint of sweetness.	Good for fish, pork, poultry, light meat game birds (such as quail and dove), and especially great with salmon.
APPLE	Slightly sweet, but dense, fruity smoke flavor.	Good for beef, poultry, game birds, pork, and ham.
CHERRY	Slightly sweet, fruity smoke flavor.	Good with all meats.
HICKORY	Pungent, smoky, bacon-like flavor, it's the most common wood used for barbecue.	Good for all smoking, especially pork and ribs; it is the most popular grilling wood in the South.
MAPLE	Mild smoky, somewhat sweet flavor.	Good with pork, poultry, cheese, vegetables, and small game birds.
MESQUITE	Strong, earthy flavor.	Good for most meats—especially beef—and most vegetables; it's the most popular grilling wood in Texas.
OAK	The second most popular wood, with a heavy smoke flavor, it's the official smoke of Texas brisket. Red oak, not yet available in pellets, is considered the best by many pit masters.	Good with red meat, pork, fish, and heavy game.
PECAN	Mild, nutty, similar to but milder than oak.	Good with any meats and known to add a more distinct smoke ring to beef.

THE FUTURE OF PELLETS

It's hard to predict what's next in pellet flavors. Special blends have become marketable for many pellet makers, but a lot of cooks like creating their own blends. Other than new blends (outlined in the chart on page 19), the newest pellet "flavor" is charcoal. If you have a soft spot for traditional backyard grill flavor, this could be what you've been looking for. These black-colored pellets are best mixed with any regular wood pellet to enhance the smoke ring on your meat (charcoal's hotter combustion atmosphere aids in the creation of a more distinct smoke ring). Charcoal pellets also feature a hotter, cleaner burn than regular wood pellets.

Ring of Fire: The Coveted Smoke Ring

Smoke rings are thought of as one of the visual hallmarks of great barbecue. The reddish-pink color that develops close to the surface of the meat is a chemical reaction created by heat, smoke, and meat. Even at lower temperature settings, wood pellets release carbon dioxide and then, combined with the charred wood, create carbon monoxide and nitrogen dioxide. Those fumes result in a chemical reaction on the surface of the meat to slowly create that iconic reddish ring. Smoke rings don't affect flavor in the least, so don't obsess over them too much. Use pecan pellets or a nitrate-rich spice rub to enhance the ring.

THE ART OF LOW-AND-SLOW SMOKING

Creating something as spectacular as smoked beef brisket is beautifully simple with a pellet smoker; however, it won't be quick. Here are the steps for a typical low-and-slow smoke:

1. Start cold—and clean. If your wood pellet grill smoker hasn't been used in a while, take a moment to remove the grate, drip pan, and heat deflector to clean out any residual ash (and extra pellets) from the cook chamber and fire pot with a shop vac.

2. Load your pellet hopper with your favorite hardwood pellet (oak is traditional for beef brisket). Replace the deflector, pans, and grate, and use your grill maker's preheating steps to ensure proper fuel flow.

3. Prep your beef. Wash your hands. When you are using smoke, great beef seasoning can be as simple as salt and pepper. It will take time for a large cut of meat like brisket to come to room temperature. Place the meat in the wood pellet grill smoker, and allow it to come fully off its chill and down to room temperature, and then up to cooking temperature (225°F in the cooking chamber). The cold meat may cause a temporary drop in your smoker temperature, but this is considered safer than leaving the meat out to come to room temperature.

4. Place your temperature probe in the center of the thickest part of the meat.

5. Wash your hands again to allow for food-safe and clean operation of machinery. (This is something you'll repeat regularly!)

FOOD-GRADE WOOD PELLET BLENDS

WOOD	BRAND(S)	FLAVOR	WHAT TO COOK WITH IT
APPLE MASH BLEND	CookinPellets	Lightly sweet blend of apple mash and hard maple	Great with light-flavor foods like chicken, pork, muffins, and cold-smoked dishes
BBQ BLEND	Pit Boss	Sweet, savory, and tart blend of maple, hickory, and cherry	Good for all foods
BOURBON BROWN SUGAR	Cabela's	Seasoned oak blend of bourbon, smoke flavor, and sweetness	Good for beef, chicken, and pork
PELLET PRO EXCLUSIVE CHARCOAL BLEND	Smoke Daddy Inc.	Charcoal blended with red oak. Mix with any flavor of wood pellets and use to enhance smoke ring (see sidebar).	Good for all meats
COMPETITION BLEND	Pit Boss, Camp Chef, Lumber Jack, Cabela's, Louisiana Grills, Mojobricks, Q Pellets, Lowe's, Field & Stream, Dick's Sporting Goods, Walmart, Home Depot, HomComfort, Griller's Gold, Kingsford, and Traeger	Blend of sweet, savory, and tart (maple, hickory, and cherry)	Good for pork, chicken, and beef
PERFECT MIX BLEND	CookinPellets	Blend of hickory, cherry, hard maple, and apple	Great on short cooks; for any foods
TEXAS BLEND	Green Mountain	Blend of oak, hickory, and mesquite	Good for all meats
REALTREE BIG GAME BLEND	Traeger	Blend of hickory, red and white oak, and rosemary	Great for venison, pheasant, and game meats
TURKEY PELLET BLEND WITH BRINE KIT	Traeger	Oak, hickory, maple, and rosemary	Turkey
TENNESSEE WHISKEY BARREL	Big Poppa Smokers, Louisiana Grills, Jack Daniels, Mr. Bar-B-Q	Aged oak from Jack Daniels Whiskey	Good for most meats

6. Adjust thermostat controls so your wood pellet grill maintains a cooking temperature of 225°F. Your brisket will need to cook at this low temperature for 1 hour and 30 minutes per pound of meat. Replenish the pellets in the hopper as needed, and allow your cook to go slowly if you want to achieve a distinct smoke ring.

7. Check and mop or spray the meat as desired. Mops and sprays are easy ways to add moisture to the surface of the meat. The liquid is typically a thinned-out version of your favorite sauce or fruit juice that is "mopped" on with a soft basting brush, or sprayed on from a reusable plastic kitchen spray bottle. Just don't open the door of the cooker more than absolutely necessary, especially during the first 1 hour and 30 minutes of cooking. Resist the urge to peek. Most wood pellet grills come with temperature probes that track the internal temperature of meat as it slowly cooks. This is a handy way to gauge progress without opening the grill.

8. When the meat reaches an internal temperature of 165°F, remind yourself that you are not done *despite* USDA recommendations! You may now opt to wrap, mop, or spritz hourly. Steady, low heat is the focus and smoke penetration is now secondary, as most of the flavor has been absorbed.

9. Many pit masters swear by using pink butcher paper over aluminum foil to wrap brisket. The "Texas Crutch" is a somewhat derogatory term for wrapping the meat in aluminum foil during the rise from 165°F to 190°F. At times, the cooking can plateau and hit a point of resistance to an increase in internal temperature. That phenomenon is called "the stall" and varies from animal to animal. Wrapping in butcher paper or foil helps to break the stall, slowly braise the meat, and accelerates the fat and collagen breakdown that becomes pure succulence. That magic really kicks in once you hit 165°F and beyond.

10. When the internal temperature hits 195°F, you can pull the roast from the wood pellet grill and allow the meat to rest for up to an hour before slicing. (Remember: The meat will continue to cook for a few minutes after being removed.) The rest period allows juices to soak into the meat rather than drain quickly due to a premature carving.

11. During the rest, take time to make sure you are properly running the pellet cooker through its important shutdown cycle so you know your smoker will be primed and ready for the next cook.

UP IN SMOKE

Smoking isn't just for preserving any more. These days, it's common to see smoked turkey and cheeses in supermarkets because people love the flavor. And, though brisket, ribs, and chicken are popular favorites, the good taste isn't limited to meats. Smoked vegetables, nuts, and even fruit are becoming mainstream delicacies.

CUTS OF BEEF AND PORK

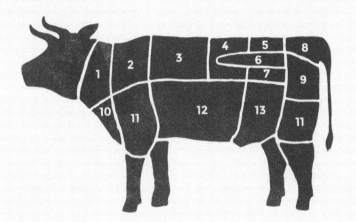

BEEF

1. Neck
2. Chuck
3. Rib
4. Short Loin
5. Sirloin
6. Tenderloin
7. Top Sirloin
8. Rump Cap
9. Round
10. Brisket
11. Shoulder Clod
12. Short Plate
13. Flank

PORK

1. Head
2. Clear Plate
3. Back Fat
4. Boston Butt/Shoulder
5. Loin
6. Ham
7. Cheek
8. Picnic Shoulder
9. Ribs
10. Bacon
11. Hock

FAVORITE FOODS TO SMOKE ON A WOOD PELLET GRILL

ITEM TO SMOKE	SMOKING TEMPERATURE	SMOKING TIME	INTERNAL TEMPERATURE	TYPE OF WOOD CHIPS
CHICKEN				
CHICKEN (BONELESS, SKINLESS)	350°F	25 to 30 minutes	170°F	Alder, pecan
CHICKEN CUT UP (LEGS/THIGHS/BREASTS)	250°F	1 hour 30 minutes to 2 hours	165°F	Cherry, pecan, oak, apple, maple
CHICKEN OR TURKEY (GROUND)	275°F	1 hour to 1 hour 30 minutes	160°F	Apple
CHICKEN WINGS	350°F	50 to 60 minutes	165°F	Hickory, oak
CHICKEN, WHOLE (3 TO 4 POUNDS)	250°F	45 minutes per pound	165°F	Cherry, pecan, oak, apple
CHICKEN HALVES	250°F	3 hours	165°F	Cherry
JERK CHICKEN LEG QUARTERS	275°F	1 hour 30 minutes	165°F	Mesquite and a few whole pimento (allspice) berries
TURKEY				
TURKEY (WHOLE)	250°F	30 minutes per pound	165°F	Apple
TURKEY LEGS	225°F	4 to 5 hours	165°F	Apple
PORK				
BABY BACK RIBS	225°F	5 hours 30 minutes to 6 hours	190°F	Hickory
BRATS	225°F	1 hour 30 minutes to 2 hours	160°F	Oak, pecan, hickory
PORK SHOULDER BOSTON BUTT (PULLED)	225°F	8 to 9 hours	205°F	Hickory
PORK SAUSAGE (GROUND)	225°F	2 hours	165°F	Apple
PORK CHOPS	325°F	45 to 50 minutes	160°F	Oak, hickory, apple
PORK LOIN ROAST	250°F	3 hours	160°F	Apple, hickory

ITEM TO SMOKE	SMOKING TEMPERATURE	SMOKING TIME	INTERNAL TEMPERATURE	TYPE OF WOOD CHIPS
PORK SPARE RIBS	250°F	6 hours	190°F	Mesquite, cherry
PORK TENDERLOIN	225°F	2 hours to 2 hours 30 minutes	160°F	Hickory, apple
BEEF				
BRISKET	225°F	1 hour to 1 hour 30 minutes	195°F to 205°F	Oak
CHUCK ROAST	225°F	1 hour per pound	120°F to 155°F	Oak, mesquite
HAMBURGERS	425°F	20 to 25 minutes	160°F	Oak
FILET MIGNON	450°F	12 to 14 minutes	120°F Rare 135°F Medium 155°F Well-done	Oak, pecan
FLANK STEAK	450°F	8 to 20 minutes	120°F Rare 135°F Medium 155°F Well-done	Any
FLAT IRON STEAK	450°F	8 to 20 minutes	120°F Rare 135°F Medium 155°F Well-done	Any
LONDON BROIL (TOP ROUND)	350°F	12 to 16 minutes	120°F Rare 135°F Medium 155°F Well-done	Any
PRIME RIB	450°F to sear, 300°F to smoke	20 minutes per pound	120°F Rare 135°F Medium 155°F Well-done	Oak, pecan
RIBEYE	450°F	8 to 20 minutes	120°F Rare 135°F Medium 155°F Well-done	Hickory, oak, mesquite

CONTINUED

FAVORITE FOODS TO SMOKE ON A WOOD PELLET GRILL CONTINUED

ITEM TO SMOKE	SMOKING TEMPERATURE	SMOKING TIME	INTERNAL TEMPERATURE	TYPE OF WOOD CHIPS
BEEF, CONTINUED				
RUMP ROAST	225°F	1 hour per pound	120°F Rare 135°F Medium 155°F Well-done	Oak, mesquite
SHORT RIBS (BEEF)	225°F	3 to 4 hours	175°F	Oak, mesquite
SIRLOIN TIP ROAST	225°F	1 hour per pound	120°F Rare 135°F Medium 155°F Well-done	Oak, mesquite
T-BONE AND PORTERHOUSE STEAKS	165°F, 450°F	45 to 50 minutes	120°F Rare 135°F Medium 155°F Well-done	Hickory
TENDERLOIN (BEEF)	400°F	25 to 30 minutes	120°F Rare 135°F Medium 155°F Well-done	Oak, hickory, pecan
TEXAS SHOULDER CLOD	250°F	12 to 16 hours	195°F	Oak
TRI-TIP	425°F	45 minutes to 1 hour	120°F Rare 135°F Medium 155°F Well-done	Oak
FISH AND SEAFOOD				
FISH (HALIBUT, SEA BASS, SWORDFISH, TROUT, AND COD)	200°F to 225°F	1 hour 30 minutes to 2 hours	140°F	Alder, apple, cherry, oak

ITEM TO SMOKE	SMOKING TEMPERATURE	SMOKING TIME	INTERNAL TEMPERATURE	TYPE OF WOOD CHIPS
OYSTERS	225°F	15 to 20 minutes	To taste	Apple, cherry, oak
SALMON	250°F	1 to 2 hours	145°F	Alder
TUNA STEAKS	250°F	1 hour	125°F	Apple, cherry, oak
FRUIT AND VEGETABLES				
BELL PEPPERS	225°F	1 hour 30 minutes	Until tender	Maple
CAULIFLOWER	200°F to 250°F	45 minutes to 1 hour 30 minutes	Until tender	Maple
CORN ON THE COB	450°F	12 to 14 minutes	Until tender	Hickory, oak, pecan, mesquite
JALAPEÑO PEPPERS	250°F	1 hour to 1 hour 30 minutes	Until tender	Maple
ONIONS	250°F	2 hours	Until tender	Maple, mesquite
PEACHES	225°F	35 to 45 minutes	To taste	Maple
PINEAPPLE	250°F	1 hour to 1 hour 30 minutes	To taste	Maple
POTATOES	400°F	1 hour 15 minutes	Until tender	Maple, pecan
SWEET POTATOES, WHOLE	375°F	1 hour to 1 hour 30 minutes	Until crispy	Maple
SQUASH AND ZUCCHINI	225°F	1 hour	Until tender	Maple

UNUSUAL FOODS TO SMOKE ON A WOOD PELLET GRILL

ITEM TO SMOKE	SMOKING TEMPERATURE	SMOKING TIME	INTERNAL TEMPERATURE	TYPE OF WOOD PELLETS
ALLIGATOR	225°F	2 hours	165°F	Mesquite
ARTICHOKES	225°F	2 hours	To taste	Maple
ASPARAGUS	240°F	1 hour	To taste	Maple
BACON OR CANDIED BACON	225°F	30 to 45 minutes	140°F	Hickory, maple
BAKED BEANS	300°F	2 hours 30 minutes to 3 hours	Until bubbly	Hickory, oak, mesquite
BEEF JERKY (THIN SLICED BEEF BOTTOM ROUND)	180°F	4 to 5 hours	To taste	Hickory
BISON BURGERS	425°F	17 to 19 minutes	140°F to 160°F	Mesquite, BBQ blend
BOLOGNA	250°F	1 hour	To taste	Hickory
BROWNIES	350°F	23 to 28 minutes	Until a toothpick inserted comes out clean	Apple, cherry
CABBAGE	240°F	2 hours	To taste	Oak, maple, apple
CAKE	350°F	1 hour	Until a toothpick inserted comes out clean	Apple, cherry
CHEESES	Under 90°F	30 to 45 minutes	To taste	Apple, hickory, mesquite
COBBLER	375°F	20 to 25 minutes	Until brown and bubbly	Apple, cherry
COOKIES	375°F	10 to 12 minutes	Until lightly browned	Alder, pecan
CORNBREAD	375°F	25 to 35 minutes	Until a toothpick inserted comes out clean	Oak, apple, pecan

ITEM TO SMOKE	SMOKING TEMPERATURE	SMOKING TIME	INTERNAL TEMPERATURE	TYPE OF WOOD PELLETS
CORNED BEEF/PASTRAMI	275°F	4 to 5 hours	185°F	Oak, hickory
CORNISH GAME HENS (APPROXIMATELY 2 1/2 POUNDS EACH)	275°F	2 to 3 hours or 45 minutes per pound	170°F	Apple
CRAB	200°F	15 minutes per pound	To taste	Oak
DUCK, WHOLE (5 POUNDS)	250°F	4 hours	165°F	Cherry, pecan
EGGPLANT	200°F	1 hour to 1 hour 30 minutes	To taste	Maple
GARLIC	225°F	2 hours	To taste	Oak
GOOSE BACON	165°F first cook, 250°F second cook	4 hours 15 minutes	To taste	Cherry
HAM, PRE-COOKED (5 TO 7 POUNDS)	275°F	5 hours	160°F	Cherry
HARD-BOILED EGGS (FOR DEVILED EGGS)	200°F	20 to 30 minutes	To taste	Hickory
ICE CREAM BREAD	350°F	50 to 60 minutes	Until a toothpick inserted comes out clean	Apple, cherry
KIELBASA SAUSAGE	225°F	1 hour 30 minutes to 2 hours	160°F	Oak, pecan, hickory
LAMB CHOPS	165°F to smoke, 450°F to sear	10 to 20 minutes	145°F	Cherry
LAMB RACK, 7 OR 8 (4-OUNCE) CHOPS CROWN (2 RACKS UPRIGHT AND TIED TOGETHER TO FORM A CROWN)	275°F	1 hour 30 minutes to 2 hours	145°F	Apple, cherry, oak

CONTINUED

UNUSUAL FOODS TO SMOKE ON A WOOD PELLET GRILL CONTINUED

ITEM TO SMOKE	SMOKING TEMPERATURE	SMOKING TIME	INTERNAL TEMPERATURE	TYPE OF WOOD PELLETS
LEG OF LAMB	325°F	20 to 25 minutes per pound	145°F	Apple, oak
LOBSTER TAIL	225°F	45 minutes to 1 hour	130° to 140°F	Alder, oak
LOX	80°F	6 hours	To taste	Alder
MAC AND CHEESE	225°F	1 hour	Until bubbly	Hickory, mesquite
MEATLOAF	225°F	2 hours	165°F	Hickory, mesquite, oak
MUFFINS	375°F	25 to 30 minutes	Until a toothpick inserted comes out clean	Apple, cherry
MUSHROOMS	225°F	1 hour 30 minutes	To taste	Oak
MUSSELS	150°F to 180°F	1 hour 30 minutes	To taste	Alder, cherry
NUTS	225°F	1 hour	To taste	Hickory, mesquite

ITEM TO SMOKE	SMOKING TEMPERATURE	SMOKING TIME	INTERNAL TEMPERATURE	TYPE OF WOOD PELLETS
PHEASANT	250°F	3 to 4 hours	160°F	Apple, cherry, hickory
QUAIL	225°F	1 hour	145°F	Hickory
SCALLOPS	225°F	25 minutes	Until opaque/firm	Cherry, oak
SHRIMP (RAW)	450°F	4 to 6 minutes	Until pink	Mesquite, hickory, pecan
SNACK MIX	225°F	2 hours to 2 hours 30 minutes	Until dry	Hickory, mesquite
TOMATOES	200°F	45 minutes	To taste	Oak
TURDUCKEN	275°F	2 hours	165°F	Oak, cherry
VENISON	225°F	1 hour 20 minutes	130° to 140°F	Hickory

MY PERFECT SMOKIN' PANTRY

Barbecue is defined differently by different people. It's a verb. It's a noun. It's a sauce. It's a type of cooking. It's even considered a flavor of potato chip! When it comes to barbecue recipes, it is often the smoke, temperatures, and cook times that create the secret ingredient. There are only a few pantry must-haves; here's what you'll find in mine:

PANTRY ESSENTIALS

★ **Allspice:** The dried black pimento berry is the key flavor behind jerk seasoning.

★ **Black pepper:** For the most vibrant flavor, always grind fresh.

★ **Bouillon cubes:** I use these to tuck concentrated umami flavor into tight spaces, like I do in my Corned Beef and Cabbage (page 88).

★ **Cajun seasoning**

★ **Cayenne pepper**

★ **Celery salt and celery seed:** The distinct flavor of these spices adds a natural punch of smoke ring–enhancing nitrite. Use them as alternatives to curing salts like Morton Tender Quick. Keep both spices on hand to control the saltiness in your rubs.

★ **Chili powder:** The trick to winning a chili cook-off is using the freshest—preferably homemade—chili powder.

★ **Coffee:** Great in rubs. I recommend stocking microground instant coffees, such as Starbucks' Via brand.

★ **Coriander (cilantro seed):** Coriander is the seed of the cilantro plant, but its flavor is not like the cilantro leaf; it tastes a bit like unsweetened Froot Loops cereal. Whole or crushed seeds round out the flavor of robust pork rubs.

★ **Cumin, ground**

★ **Garlic, powdered**

★ **Ginger, powdered**

★ **Mustard, dry**

★ **Onions, dried:** Dried onions can easily be rehydrated and used for steaming small burgers or as a condiment. They can also add strong flavor to rubs and marinades.

★ **Paprika, sweet and smoked**

★ **Red pepper flakes:** A little bit goes a long way, but it kicks up flavor.

★ **Salt, curing:** Morton Tender Quick is a venerable brand. Also known as pink salt, Prague powder, or Insta Cure, curing salt will also artificially enhance a smoke ring.

★ **Salt, kosher:** Stick to your favorite name brand to control recipe consistency.

★ **Sugar, turbinado:** This is also known as raw sugar (see sidebar, page 31).

 *Barbecue IQ: Sugar*

Not all sugar is created equal (no pun intended). Most barbecue smoking rub and sauce recipes call for brown sugar because it adds a deeper flavor to the meat. While you can use regular light or dark brown sugar (which is really just white sugar with added molasses), many pit masters prefer turbinado sugar (a.k.a. raw sugar) because its larger crystals add a welcome texture to robust rubs. Bonus: It's less processed and stands up well to heat.

Sugars and sweet sauces are normally added at the very end of high-heat grilling for caramelization, but because you'll typically stick with low-and-slow temperatures when smoking, adding them earlier shouldn't be a problem. Word of caution: Sugar has a scorch point (when it burns) of just above 330°F, so you'll want to watch out for that when using your wood pellet grill's higher heat settings.

SECRET SAUCE STAPLES

Some pit master purists don't allow sauces at their tables. I understand this, because it can sometimes seem like a crime to cover up the pure wood smoke flavors you achieve with pellet power. Still, sauces have joys of their own. Here are a few sauce ingredient staples:

★ **Ketchup:** You probably have a favorite brand—just watch out for the quality and quantity of sugar. Many cheaper ketchups contain high-fructose corn syrup (sometimes labeled as corn sugar) in their ingredients. Try to stick with a brand that doesn't contain this processed ingredient.

★ **Mustard:** In smoking prep, you can use mustard as a no-fuss adherent for rubs. Keep it simple and stick with cheap yellow table mustard, unless otherwise directed in a recipe. It's also the base for South Carolina-style sauces.

★ **Vinegar:** Apple cider vinegar provides a tart punch to a sauce recipe. It plays a starring role in North Carolina-style barbecue sauces.

★ **Worcestershire sauce:** Only use high-quality brands, because the punch behind its flavor comes from anchovies; generics often skip the fish.

LET'S COOK OUT

Wood pellet grills are still pretty rare in the wild, so expect your magic smoker to be a great conversation starter at your next cookout. You will feel like a combination of scientist, gadget guru, and chef. Plus, with the lack of flareups, you'll be able to safely cook more servings without fighting flames. You will appear cool when easily tending to the grill and, later, be even revered when your friends taste your delicious food.

COOKOUT TIPS

With proper planning and plenty of time, you can consolidate a menu and cook several recipes at once. Here are a few tips to maximize your pellet-powered cookout:

★ Orchestrate a detailed timeline for your smoking day. This should culminate with the reveal of your centerpiece meat as your friends and family are just getting settled in. Don't forget to account for the meat's resting time.

★ Serve it hot. Take care with the resting process and be sure you still serve your dish hot. Hot food pulls in more senses like smell. For example, nothing is better than hot pizza—even cheap pizza! That steaming slice on the ride home is as good as it gets. Hot food gets people's attention on a primal level.

★ Use secondary grill shelves as a staging area for appetizers with shorter cook times. Quick-cooking veggies can be added last and will hold until serving.

★ Avoid peeking and allow for extra cook time when adding cold food alongside items already cooking in the pellet grill.

★ Allow for good smoke flow across your entire grate surface. Avoid crowding the food, and leave 1 to 2 inches of space surrounding food pieces.

★ Rib racks are affordable and can save large amounts of cook space. They are a must if you regularly smoke ribs for a crowd.

★ Say yes when somebody asks, "Is there something I can do to help?" One of the greatest assists can be a help with cleanup. Be ready if they ask, "Is there anything we can bring?" Some ideas include chips, condiments, ice, or a cooler of beverages. Most guests enjoy contributing, so make them feel good!

★ Because wood pellet grill smokers offer high temperatures in addition to low, you can make some things quickly or in advance, such as appetizers, smoked nuts and cheeses, and desserts. Of course, when cooking for a really large crowd, it might help if you cook or finish a couple of side dishes in the oven or have a neighbor bring over an extra grill.

COOKOUT MENUS

OYSTER ROAST BBQ

Delicious Deviled Crab Appetizer, page 110

Roasted Oysters on the Half Shell with Compound Butter, page 114

Baby Back Ribs with Bill's Best BBQ Sauce, page 64

Spatchcocked Quail with Smoked Fruit, page 142

Southern Slaw, page 156

Carolina Baked Beans, page 158

Sweet Cheese Muffins, page 169

Smoked Blackberry Pie, page 173

MEMORIAL DAY PICNIC

Bill's Best French Onion Burgers, page 86

Savory-Sweet Turkey Legs, page 52

Charred Shrimp Skewers, page 119

Twice-Smoked Potatoes, page 150

Broccoli-Cauliflower Salad, page 153

S'mores Dip Skillet, page 172

LOWCOUNTRY BACKYARD WEDDING

Charleston Crab Cakes with Remoulade, page 106

Simple Cream Cheese Sausage Balls, page 71

Pig Pops, page 69

Spicy BBQ Pecans, page 178

Creamy Lowcountry Shrimp and Grits, page 118

Lobster Tails in Garlic Butter Sauce, page 116

Smoked Prime Rib, page 96

Brussels Sprout Bites with Cilantro-Balsamic Drizzle, page 155

Caprese Salad with Cold-Smoked Mozzarella, page 170

LABOR DAY BLOCK PARTY

Bacon-Wrapped Jalapeño Poppers, page 163

Seasoned Tuna Steaks, page 117

Jamaican Jerk Chicken Quarters, page 53

Pineapple-Pepper Pork Kebabs, page 70

Mexican Street Corn with Chipotle Butter, page 149

Potluck Salad with Smoked Cornbread, page 160

Bacon Chocolate Chip Cookies, page 171

CHRISTMAS IN CAROLINA

Smoked Christmas Crown Roast of Lamb, page 141

Mini Turducken Roulade, page 50

Ultimate Brisket, page 100

Quattro Formaggi Macaroni and Cheese, page 179

Roasted Okra, page 151

Georgia Sweet Onion Bake, page 157

BLT Pasta Salad, page 159

Carrot Cake on the Barbie, page 174

CHEERS

Smoked meats and cheeses pair nicely with a great adult beverage, be it beer, whiskey, wine, a cocktail—or even champagne! Just like great whiskey and wine, good barbecue takes time, too. Proper aging, wood barrels, and sometimes even charcoal create a unique kinship between meal and beverage. Food always tastes better with a good drink. Beauty is in the eye of the beer holder.

If you are looking to pair your barbecue with the perfect beverage, here are a few suggestions:

★ Beer is my barbecue "go-to," as the light carbonation and drinkability make for a satisfying and refreshing swig. Plus, there is a type of brew for all tastes. If spicy Jamaican Jerk Chicken Quarters (page 53) are on the grill, opt for an amber ale or a pale Jamaican lager such as Red Stripe. Heartier meats, like brisket and sauced meats, can withstand stronger brews such as a dark lager, an IPA, or a brown ale. I like to match strength with strength.

★ Whiskey is a Southern favorite. Pulled pork pairs nicely with a Tennessee whiskey, with its hint of charcoal. If you're dining on a slab of smoked spare ribs or the Pig Pops (page 69) try a woody Jim Beam Black bourbon (on the rocks), aged for years in oak barrels, to help cut the fatty pork.

★ Red wine is a great choice for pairing with burgers, all beef dishes, and even barbecue ribs. A bold red California Cabernet is my favorite.

★ White wines are a solid choice for your pellet-smoked salmon because the fish's oily texture needs enough acidity to cut through the fat. Look for a light, dry, and crisp white.

★ With mixed drinks and cocktails, you'll want to keep things bubbly with a vodka-and-lime-based spritzer. Add a grilled theme to your fruit garnish by grilling pineapple or citrus slices just enough to show a bit of a char. If you are mixing drinks for a crowd, a red wine sangria dispenser will always get fully drained!

★ Champagne has a special relationship with barbecue; it is often cited as the perfect pairing because of its bubbles—so much so that "bubble-cue" events have become common at swanky food festivals. The effervescence cuts through the fatty and salty richness to delightfully wash down every smoky bite.

PARTING TIPS

With new grilling gadgets and wood pellet grill advancements popping up every year, I'll be sure to track modern hacks and clever ideas at BarbecueTricks.com. Here are a few last tips to get you smokin':

Sweet finish: Hold sweet sauces until the end of your cook because sugar burns quickly. Consider cutting out the sugar or just serving sauce as an optional side. There's an old saying, "Taste the flavor in the meat when the sauce is on the side."

Back to the grind: Eliminate boring black pepper shakers. Grinding your own fresh whole black peppercorns will add next-level flavor, guaranteed.

Convection: The convection oven–like qualities of your pellet grill are unique in the barbecue world. The even heat and circulation may reduce cook times for recipes designed for other types of smokers.

Tongs, not forks: You don't want to pierce, puncture, or prick the exterior surface of your barbecue, especially sausage and poultry, because that will drain out those fabulous and flavorful juices from the meat. Use that long barbecue fork for a tent spike instead. Seriously, jam it into the ground and use it to secure your tailgating tent! Just don't use it on meat and drain those flavorful juices if you don't have to.

Fire safety: Have a dedicated fire extinguisher on hand that is rated for grease fires as well as wood, and be ready to use it. Most competitions require you to have one at your cook site, and they're not expensive. We keep the best deals updated on our resource page at BarbecueTricks.com.

Shut it down: Remember to shut down your pellet grill using the manufacturer's recommended process. This method will burn out excess pellets so your grill's fire pot is empty and safely ready for the next cook.

Part Two
IT'S SMOKIN' TIME

Chapter 3
POULTRY

Both backyard chefs and hard-core competition barbecue teams like wood pellet grills for their ability to smoke fowl, such as chicken and turkey, to perfection. By cooking low and slow with hardwood pellet smoke, the skin of your poultry gets plenty of time for the fat to render (and with duck there's plenty of flavorful fat). As the poultry smokes, it also bastes itself slowly. Plus, the more delicate meat showcases subtle fruitwood smoke flavors nicely. When you see pink, don't panic. As long as the juices run clear and you verify with a good thermometer that your bird is not bleeding, it's smokin'!

One of the best things about smoking poultry is the price. Pound for pound, there is no protein more affordable than chicken leg quarters. But even if you pay a bit more for the breast meat, you won't be disappointed. The smoke flavor takes the healthy, sometimes boring boneless breast to heavenly new hickory heights! ◊

◀ WILD WEST WINGS, page 59

CUTS

Turkey, chicken, and duck each have their own power cuts, but they are all a perfect match for your wood pellet grill.

★ **Breast meat** is like a blank canvas for flavors. It's delicate, lean, and clean, and is the top choice for many health-conscious diners. Note that the breast is also the easiest to dry out, so smoke with care.

★ **Thighs** are a favorite on smokers because, unlike breasts, they take much longer to dry out. Thighs are actually difficult to overcook. That, along with their relatively inexpensive price, makes them an easy choice for feeding a crowd.

★ The **drumsticks or legs** are Mother Nature's food on a stick! They are a top cookout choice, especially when kids are at the table.

★ **Wings** have come a long way. They used to be a budget cut of meat but over the years have become a tailgate obsession. If you are feeding a large group, be sure to separate whole wings into wingettes (the "flat" two-bone section) and the drumettes. It's interesting to observe that everyone has a personal preference.

★ You should also consider smoking the **whole bird**, although it's technically the opposite of a cut. A roast turkey or chicken makes for a table centerpiece that is as beautiful as it is delicious. Just take care not to overcook the breast meat before the thighs are done.

TECHNIQUES

Your wood pellet grill will handle most of the hard work for poultry, but there are a few techniques you might want to try in your attempt to reach pit master perfection. The main techniques for turkey and chicken include *brining, injecting, seasoning,* and *dry brining*.

★ For **brining**, use what many people consider to be a universal ratio of salt to water: one gallon of water mixed with one cup of kosher salt. You may initially use hot water to dissolve the salt and/or sugar (if you're using that), but always keep the meat and brine solution chilled to prevent food contamination.

★ When **injecting**, take care to insert the injector needle into the meat via the *interior* of the cavity and rib cage. This way, you won't pierce or blemish the outer skin, so it will hold in juices just as the food gods intended.

★ When **seasoning** the whole bird or most individual cuts, I make an effort to carefully peel back the skin and rub seasonings *underneath* it and into the muscles in all parts of the bird. It

 **Turkey Double Take**

You know you normally have half a turkey left over anyway, so why bust your grill with a 20-pound turkey when you could smoke two 12-pound birds? This way, you get *twice* the drumsticks and *double* the smoky surface area, and you'll dramatically reduce your cook time.

takes a little extra effort, but by doing this you'll get salt and real flavor into the meat. Poultry skin—especially thick turkey skin—is akin to a wetsuit. You want to season it, but the seasoning won't penetrate the skin.

★ **Dry brining** is a technique that I use to help create a crisp chicken skin you can bite through. It involves rubbing a dry seasoning, mostly salt, over and under the skin of the bird. Then you let it dry uncovered in the refrigerator for four hours before blotting completely dry with paper towels and cooking. The final result is a well-seasoned, crispy treat.

SPATCHCOCKING

Another way to trim your poultry is by using a butterflying technique called spatchcocking. This can be a slippery task, but it's definitely not complicated. Simply use a heavy pair of kitchen shears to cut out the spine of the bird. You'll scissor completely through the skin up and down each side of the spine. Then open and flatten the full carcass skin-side up on the grill grate, cracking or splitting the small breast bone in the middle. The bigger the bird, the tougher the task; just take care to start and finish with thoroughly sanitized scissors and hands. The newfound surface area will now allow the bird to absorb twice the smoke flavor. It will be easier to carve, and it looks extra cool on the grate of your wood pellet grill.

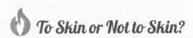

To Skin or Not to Skin?

Skin is always a consideration when dealing with poultry. My suggestion is to leave it on. The heat from a wood pellet fire easily blasts through rubbery skin; however, poultry skin *can* often get a leathery texture when it's slow-smoked. To promote crisp skin, use the dry brining technique. With a little extra time, you can finally achieve crispy skin on your bird!

CLEANING

Do you need to wash your bird? These days, many barbecue gurus say it is not necessary, because having raw poultry come in additional contact with your cleaning area will invite increased danger of bacterial contamination. Call me squeamish, but I *always* wash the exterior and interior of poultry before seasoning. It's also a great time to remove any extras stuffed inside the cavity, like gizzards and giblets. (If your bird has one of those pop thermometers, you can leave it in and use it, as your wood pellet grill temperature will be controlled much like a home oven.)

RULES TO GRILL BY

Here are a few pro tips to perfect your smoked poultry skills:

★ Since we do much of our meat shopping in supermarkets, you'll want to read the packaging for any indication that the bird may have been pre-brined or enhanced with salt water. Added salt water is not a bad thing, but doing this will simply help you know if you're paying by the pound for chicken or for chicken swelled with heavy liquid and other preservatives. Plus, you'll be able to more precisely control your recipe's salt quantity.

★ Poultry is more prone to contamination than other meats such as beef. Use extra care to avoid foodborne pathogens such as salmonella by regularly washing your hands while cooking and after handling raw meat. Also, make sure to keep raw poultry (and any residual liquid) away from ready-to-serve smoked meats. Sanitize everything that comes into contact with raw poultry before reusing it, including the sink, counter, cutting board, knives, and utensils.

★ So much of barbecue and grilling prep is done outdoors during the summer months. That's an atmosphere ripe for bacteria growth. Be sure you keep your marinating meat cold. Always marinate in the refrigerator and never reuse marinades.

★ The only real way to know if your bird is safely cooked is to break out a meat thermometer and take the internal temperature of the thickest part of the meat. Avoid probing next to bone or out through the other side of the cut. An internal temperature of 165°F is a must.

★ As mentioned previously, thick turkey and chicken skin won't allow seasoning to penetrate. Make a plan to carefully season under the skin using your fingers. It's easier to do than you think; just put the skin back in place once you're done.

ASIAGO-SPINACH HASSELBACK CHICKEN

Serves 4

BRINING TIME: 2 HOURS
PREP TIME: 25 MINUTES
SMOKE TIME: 25 TO 30 MINUTES

 SMOKE
TEMPERATURE:
350°F

 WOOD PELLETS:
HICKORY OR
TEXAS BLEND

FOR THE BRINE

¼ cup salt

¼ cup packed light
brown sugar

6 cups water

4 boneless, skinless
chicken breasts

**FOR THE STUFFING
AND CHICKEN**

1 cup grated Asiago cheese

1 cup torn fresh spinach leaves

8 ounces cream cheese,
softened

1 tablespoon minced garlic

2 teaspoons salt

1 tablespoon plus 1 teaspoon
freshly ground black
pepper, divided

2 teaspoons poultry seasoning

2 teaspoons garlic powder

2 teaspoons onion powder

Do kids these days know who Popeye is? In the '60s, the spinach-gobbling sailor was a fixture on TV. He made me and many others a fan of spinach. Interestingly, the leafy green used to simply be known as the "Spanish vegetable." That moniker was later shortened to its current name. In this recipe, the spinach and cheese make a delicious stuffing for often ho-hum chicken breasts. It's good for you, too, and as a grown-up, I like the health benefits of spinach. It's packed with nutrients, including potassium, magnesium, vitamin K, and especially iron. Plus it's good for muscle growth. Just ask Popeye!

TO MAKE THE BRINE

1. In a large bowl, combine the salt and brown sugar with 6 cups of water, stirring to dissolve.

2. Add the chicken breasts to the brine, cover, and refrigerate for 2 hours.

3. Remove the chicken from the brine, rinse it, and discard the brine.

TO MAKE THE STUFFING AND CHICKEN

1. Supply your smoker with wood pellets and follow the manufacturer's specific start-up procedure. Preheat, with the lid closed, to 350°F.

2. In a bowl, stir together the Asiago cheese, spinach leaves, cream cheese, minced garlic, salt, and 2 teaspoons of pepper; set aside.

3. Cut parallel lines horizontally down the length of each chicken breast to create the "Hasselback" style: deep cuts, but not all the way through the chicken.

4. In another bowl, mix together the poultry seasoning, remaining 2 teaspoons of pepper, the garlic powder, and onion powder to form a rub, and season the chicken well with it.

5. Slather the spinach–cream cheese mixture inside each incision in the breasts, using up all of the mixture.

6. Place the chicken breasts in a cast iron skillet on the grill, close the lid, and smoke for 25 to 30 minutes, or until the juices run clear and a meat thermometer inserted in the thickest part of the meat reads 170°F.

Ingredient Tip Avoid Popeye's canned greens and use organic fresh spinach in this dish for the best texture and flavor.

BEER CAN-SMOKED CHICKEN

Serves 3 to 4

PREP TIME: 30 MINUTES

SMOKE TIME: 3 TO 4 HOURS

 SMOKE
TEMPERATURE:
250°F

 WOOD PELLETS:
APPLE, HICKORY,
OAK, OR PECAN

FOR THE INJECTION AND RUB

8 tablespoons (1 stick) unsalted butter, melted

½ cup apple cider vinegar

½ cup Cajun seasoning, divided

1 teaspoon garlic powder

1 teaspoon onion powder

1 (4-pound) whole chicken, giblets removed

Extra-virgin olive oil, for rubbing

1 (12-ounce) can beer

FOR THE MOP SAUCE

1 cup apple juice

½ cup extra-virgin olive oil

The hardest thing about this recipe and technique is keeping your balance. Not because you're probably drinking beer while you're cooking, but because it's important to balance your chicken on the beer can *carefully*, using the legs to create a sturdy tripod. Your injection will add more flavor than any of the liquid in the can. Try to inject from the inside of the cavity of the bird to keep the outer skin unblemished.

TO MAKE THE INJECTION AND RUB

1. In a small bowl, whisk together the butter, vinegar, ¼ cup of Cajun seasoning, garlic powder, and onion powder.

2. Use a meat-injecting syringe to inject the liquid into various spots in the chicken. Inject about half of the mixture into the breasts and the other half throughout the rest of the chicken.

3. Rub the chicken all over with olive oil and apply the remaining ¼ cup of Cajun seasoning, being sure to rub under the skin as well.

4. Drink or discard half the beer and place the opened beer can on a stable surface.

5. Place the bird's cavity on top of the can and position the chicken so it will sit up by itself. Prop the legs forward to make the bird more stable, or buy an inexpensive, specially made stand to hold the beer can and chicken in place.

TO MAKE THE MOP SAUCE AND SMOKE THE CHICKEN

1. Supply your smoker with wood pellets and follow the manufacturer's specific start-up procedure. Preheat, with the lid closed, to 250°F.

2. In a clean 12-ounce spray bottle, combine the apple juice and olive oil. Cover and shake the mop sauce well before each use.

3. Carefully put the chicken on the grill. Close the lid and smoke the chicken for 3 to 4 hours, spraying with the mop sauce every hour, until golden brown and a meat thermometer inserted in the thickest part of the thigh reads 165°F. Keep a piece of aluminum foil handy to loosely cover the chicken if the skin begins to brown too quickly.

4. Let the meat rest for 5 minutes before carving.

Substitution Tip The mop sauce helps keep the bird moist, but you are not limited to using apple juice. Apple cider vinegar, orange juice, or a mix of both would also work nicely. But be careful: The more sugar you add to the mop, the more you'll need to watch out for burning.

BUFFALO CHICKEN WRAPS

Serves 4

PREP TIME: 30 MINUTES

SMOKE TIME: 20 MINUTES

 SMOKE
TEMPERATURE:
350°F

 WOOD PELLETS:
HICKORY OR OAK

2 teaspoons poultry seasoning

1 teaspoon freshly ground
black pepper

1 teaspoon garlic powder

1 to 1½ pounds chicken tenders

4 tablespoons (½ stick)
unsalted butter, melted

½ cup hot sauce (such as
Frank's RedHot)

4 (10-inch) flour tortillas

1 cup shredded lettuce

½ cup diced tomato

½ cup diced celery

½ cup diced red onion

½ cup shredded
Cheddar cheese

¼ cup blue cheese crumbles

¼ cup prepared ranch dressing

2 tablespoons sliced pickled
jalapeño peppers (optional)

The origin of Buffalo sauce goes back to 1964, to the Anchor Bar in Buffalo, New York. It is really the easiest sauce to make. It's simply hot sauce and melted butter. If you want to get really traditional, avoid Tabasco and use Texas Pete or Frank's RedHot in this recipe.

1. Supply your smoker with wood pellets and follow the manufacturer's specific start-up procedure. Preheat, with the lid closed, to 350°F.

2. In a small bowl, stir together the poultry seasoning, pepper, and garlic powder to create an all-purpose rub, and season the chicken tenders with it.

3. Arrange the tenders directly on the grill, close the lid, and smoke for 20 minutes, or until a meat thermometer inserted in the thickest part of the meat reads 170°F.

4. In another bowl, stir together the melted butter and hot sauce and coat the smoked chicken with it.

5. To serve, heat the tortillas on the grill for less than a minute on each side and place on a plate.

6. Top each tortilla with some of the lettuce, tomato, celery, red onion, Cheddar cheese, blue cheese crumbles, ranch dressing, and jalapeños (if using).

7. Divide the chicken among the tortillas, close up securely, and serve.

Ingredient Tip Only add hot sauce—that is, hot in temperature— to hot food, or in the case of this recipe, warmed hot sauce. The "warm sauce on hot meat" rule helps keep meat from seizing up and becoming tough. Plus, the risk of foodborne germs is generally reduced if the sauce has been heated through.

DUCK A L'SMOKER WITH MANDARIN GLAZE

Serves 3 to 4

BRINING TIME: 4 TO 6 HOURS
PREP TIME: 20 MINUTES
SMOKE TIME: 4 HOURS

 SMOKE
TEMPERATURE:
250°F

 WOOD PELLETS:
CHERRY OR PECAN

1 quart buttermilk

1 (5-pound) whole duck

¾ cup soy sauce

½ cup hoisin sauce

½ cup rice wine vinegar

2 tablespoons sesame oil

1 tablespoon freshly ground
black pepper

1 tablespoon minced garlic

Mandarin Glaze (page 188),
for drizzling

Duck is a notoriously fatty bird. The low, slow cook time here allows for maximum smoke and fat rendering. In fact, you'll need to break my usual rule of *not* piercing poultry skin! With duck, you'll be poking the skin (not the meat), with a fork to allow for easier rendering. Before you start, trim off and reserve as much of that extra fat in the cavity, on the skin, and around the neck of the duck as possible. Render it later for delicacies such as duck-fat fries.

1. With a very sharp knife, remove as much fat from the duck as you can. Refrigerate or freeze the fat for later use.

2. Pour the buttermilk into a large container with a lid and submerge the whole duck in it. Cover and let brine in the refrigerator for 4 to 6 hours.

3. Supply your smoker with wood pellets and follow the manufacturer's specific start-up procedure. Preheat, with the lid closed, to 250°F.

4. Remove the duck from the buttermilk brine, then rinse it and pat dry with paper towels.

5. In a bowl, combine the soy sauce, hoisin sauce, vinegar, sesame oil, pepper, and garlic to form a paste. Reserve ¼ cup for basting.

6. Poke holes in the skin of the duck and rub the remaining paste all over and inside the cavity.

7. Place the duck on the grill breast-side down, close the lid, and smoke for about 4 hours, basting every hour with the reserved paste, until a meat thermometer inserted in the thickest part of the meat reads 165°F. Use aluminum foil to tent the duck in the last 30 minutes or so if it starts to brown too quickly.

8. To finish, drizzle with glaze.

Substitution Tip I love the flavor of hoisin sauce, but if you don't want to buy a jar just for this recipe, feel free to use teriyaki sauce instead.

EASY RAPID-FIRE ROAST CHICKEN

Serves 3 to 4

PREP TIME: 10 MINUTES

SMOKE TIME: 1 HOUR TO 1 HOUR 30 MINUTES

 SMOKE TEMPERATURE: 450°F

 WOOD PELLETS: APPLE OR PECAN

1 (4-pound) whole chicken, giblets removed

Extra-virgin olive oil, for rubbing

3 tablespoons Greek seasoning

Juice of 1 lemon

Butcher's string

The beauty of the wood pellet grill is that it can smoke either low and slow or hot and fast with the flip of a switch. This is a time-saving recipe for roast chicken—it's almost as easy as buying a cooked rotisserie chicken at the market, but better.

1. Supply your smoker with wood pellets and follow the manufacturer's specific start-up procedure. Preheat, with the lid closed, to 450°F.

2. Rub the bird generously all over with oil, including inside the cavity.

3. Sprinkle the Greek seasoning all over and under the skin of the bird, and squeeze the lemon juice over the breast.

4. Tuck the chicken wings behind the back and tie the legs together with butcher's string or cooking twine.

5. Put the chicken directly on the grill, breast-side up, close the lid, and roast for 1 hour to 1 hour 30 minutes, or until a meat thermometer inserted in the thigh reads 165°F.

6. Let the meat rest for 10 minutes before carving.

Ingredient Tip The seasoning possibilities are endless here. Try Cajun, chipotle, Italian, or adobo seasoning, or create your own.

CINCO DE MAYO CHICKEN ENCHILADAS

Serves 6

PREP TIME: 15 MINUTES
SMOKE TIME: 45 MINUTES

 SMOKE
TEMPERATURE:
350°F

 WOOD PELLETS:
MESQUITE

6 cups diced cooked chicken

3 cups grated Monterey Jack cheese, divided

1 cup sour cream

1 (4-ounce) can chopped green chiles

2 (10-ounce) cans red or green enchilada sauce, divided

12 (8-inch) flour tortillas

½ cup chopped scallions

¼ cup chopped fresh cilantro

Cinco de Mayo celebrates the Mexican victory over French forces during the 1862 Battle of Puebla. These days, we mark the occasion with parties, tequila, and, of course, great food. Adding some mesquite smoke makes this an enchilada bake you'll want to go back to more than just one day a year.

1. Supply your smoker with wood pellets and follow the manufacturer's specific start-up procedure. Preheat, with the lid closed, to 350°F.

2. In a large bowl, combine the cooked chicken, 2 cups of cheese, the sour cream, and green chiles to make the filling.

3. Pour one can of enchilada sauce in the bottom of a 9-by-13-inch baking dish or aluminum pan.

4. Spoon ⅓ cup of the filling on each tortilla and roll up securely.

5. Transfer the tortillas seam-side down to the baking dish, then pour the remaining can of enchilada sauce over them, coating all exposed surfaces of the tortillas.

6. Sprinkle the remaining 1 cup of cheese over the enchiladas and cover tightly with aluminum foil.

7. Bake on the grill, with the lid closed, for 30 minutes, then remove the foil.

8. Continue baking with the lid closed for 15 minutes, or until bubbly.

9. Garnish the enchiladas with the chopped scallions and cilantro and serve immediately.

Ingredient Tip Red enchilada sauce is made with red chiles and tomato. Some people prefer a green enchilada sauce, made from green chiles and tomatillos. If you're hunting for heat, you'll want to go green, and if you like it extra-spicy, add jalapeños to the blend.

MINI TURDUCKEN ROULADE

Serves 6

PREP TIME: 20 MINUTES

SMOKE TIME: 2 HOURS

 SMOKE
TEMPERATURE:
275°F

 WOOD PELLETS:
OAK OR CHERRY

1 (16-ounce) boneless
turkey breast

1 (8- to 10-ounce) boneless
duck breast

1 (8-ounce) boneless, skinless
chicken breast

Salt

Freshly ground black pepper

2 cups Italian dressing

2 tablespoons Cajun seasoning

1 cup prepared seasoned
stuffing mix

8 slices bacon

Butcher's string

Turducken is a Cajun specialty. Sure, you *could* start with a
30-pound turkey and de-bone all the birds, or you can make
things much easier by using boneless breasts like I do here. This
makes for an easy mini *roulade*, a French word meaning a dish
cooked in the form of a roll with a soft filling. If you still think it's
too much trouble, call your butcher. You can occasionally find a
raw turducken roast at the grocery store, where all the work has
been done for you, or you can order one online.

1. Butterfly the turkey, duck, and chicken breasts, cover with plastic wrap
   and, using a mallet, flatten each ½ inch thick.

2. Season all the meat on both sides with a little salt and pepper.

3. In a medium bowl, combine the Italian dressing and Cajun seasoning.
   Spread one-fourth of the mixture on top of the flattened turkey breast.

4. Place the duck breast on top of the turkey, spread it with one-fourth of
   the dressing mixture, and top with the stuffing mix.

5. Place the chicken breast on top of the duck and spread with
   one-fourth of the dressing mixture.

6. Supply your smoker with wood pellets and follow the manufacturer's
   specific start-up procedure. Preheat, with the lid closed, to 275°F.

7. Tightly roll up the stack, tie with butcher's string, and slather the whole
   thing with the remaining dressing mixture.

8. Wrap the bacon slices around the turducken and secure with toothpicks, or try making a bacon weave (see the technique for this in the
   Jalapeño-Bacon Pork Tenderloin recipe on page 75).

9. Place the turducken roulade in a roasting pan. Transfer to the grill,
   close the lid, and roast for 2 hours, or until a meat thermometer
   inserted in the turducken reads 165°F. Tent with aluminum foil in
   the last 30 minutes, if necessary, to keep from overbrowning.

10. Let the turducken rest for 15 to 20 minutes before carving.
    Serve warm.

Pair It **Try serving with a Watermelon-Berry Bowl (page 162).**

SMOKE-ROASTED CHICKEN THIGHS

Serves 4 to 6

MARINATING TIME: 1 HOUR

PREP TIME: 5 MINUTES

SMOKE TIME: 1 HOUR 30 MINUTES TO 2 HOURS

 SMOKE TEMPERATURE: 250°F

 WOOD PELLETS: PECAN OR OAK

3 pounds chicken thighs

2 teaspoons salt

2 teaspoons freshly ground black pepper

2 teaspoons garlic powder

2 teaspoons onion powder

2 cups prepared Italian dressing

Chicken thighs are an easy win on the grill for several reasons. They are fatty and delicious, super affordable, and almost impossible to overcook and dry out. Many pit masters keep the seasoning simple by using their favorite salad dressing as a marinade.

1. Place the chicken thighs in a shallow dish and sprinkle with the salt, pepper, garlic powder, and onion powder, being sure to get under the skin.

2. Cover with the Italian dressing, coating all sides, and refrigerate for 1 hour.

3. Supply your smoker with wood pellets and follow the manufacturer's specific start-up procedure. Preheat, with the lid closed, to 250°F.

4. Remove the chicken thighs from the marinade and place directly on the grill, skin-side down. Discard the marinade.

5. Close the lid and roast the chicken for 1 hour 30 minutes to 2 hours, or until a meat thermometer inserted in the thickest part of the thighs reads 165°F. Do not turn the thighs during the smoking process.

Ingredient Tip Competition barbecue pit masters obsess over chicken thigh preparation. They take great effort to remove and trim the underside of the skin. It's a meticulous process of surgically shaving with a razor blade and delicately scraping. Then they replace the skin and, to smoke, they divide the chicken pieces among the cups of a muffin pan to ensure that they're uniformly shaped with bite-through consistency. You won't need to go through that much trouble to impress your guests, but do take some extra time to trim off excess fat and allow for a bit of seasoning to get under the skin.

SAVORY-SWEET TURKEY LEGS

Makes 4 legs

BRINING TIME: OVERNIGHT
PREP TIME: 10 MINUTES
SMOKE TIME: 4 TO 5 HOURS

 SMOKE
TEMPERATURE:
225°F

 WOOD PELLETS:
APPLE

1 gallon hot water

1 cup curing salt (such as
Morton Tender Quick)

¼ cup packed light
brown sugar

1 teaspoon freshly ground
black pepper

1 teaspoon ground cloves

1 bay leaf

2 teaspoons liquid smoke

4 turkey legs

Mandarin Glaze (page 188),
for serving

When it comes to fair food, the turkey leg is king of food-on-a-stick. I've learned that, sadly, almost all fair, festival, and commercial turkey legs come from food purveyors *precooked* and frozen. The good news is you can find them fresh in smaller quantities at the mega-superstores I like to refer to as "Wallyworld." Turkey legs are really inexpensive, and nothing beats preparing them low-and-slow on a wood pellet grill smoker. The tough meat and tendons really benefit from the long cook.

1. In a large container with a lid, stir together the water, curing salt, brown sugar, pepper, cloves, bay leaf, and liquid smoke until the salt and sugar are dissolved; let come to room temperature.

2. Submerge the turkey legs in the seasoned brine, cover, and refrigerate overnight.

3. When ready to smoke, remove the turkey legs from the brine and rinse them; discard the brine.

4. Supply your smoker with wood pellets and follow the manufacturer's specific start-up procedure. Preheat, with the lid closed, to 225°F.

5. Arrange the turkey legs on the grill, close the lid, and smoke for 4 to 5 hours, or until dark brown and a meat thermometer inserted in the thickest part of the meat reads 165°F.

6. Serve with Mandarin Glaze on the side or drizzled over the turkey legs.

Ingredient Tip Curing salt often used on meats to add texture, flavor, and color (a hot dog wouldn't be that lovely pink without similar cures). Use it instead of table salt in this brine to give the turkey a succulent, ham-like texture.

JAMAICAN JERK CHICKEN QUARTERS

Serves 4

PREP TIME: 15 MINUTES

SMOKE TIME: 1 HOUR TO
1 HOUR 30 MINUTES

 SMOKE
TEMPERATURE:
275°F

 WOOD PELLETS:
MESQUITE

4 chicken leg quarters, scored

¼ cup canola oil

½ cup Jamaican Jerk Paste
(page 189)

1 tablespoon whole allspice
(pimento) berries

Jamaican Jerk cuisine has a couple of standard traits. Your recipe needs Scotch bonnet peppers to give it a spice kick, and you have to grill over pimento wood. Unfortunately, both Scotch bonnets and pimento wood are hard to find in the United States. Habanero peppers are close enough (found in the paste) and we sneak in the pimento wood flavor via dried pimento berries, also known as allspice. Add a handful to the mesquite pellets in the bottom of your hopper (or in a smoker tube). The fantastic aroma is a combination of spices like cloves, cinnamon, nutmeg, and ginger, thus its name—allspice.

1. Supply your smoker with wood pellets and follow the manufacturer's specific start-up procedure. Preheat, with the lid closed, to 275°F.

2. Brush the chicken with canola oil, then brush 6 tablespoons of the Jerk paste on and under the skin. Reserve the remaining 2 tablespoons of paste for basting.

3. Throw the whole allspice berries in with the wood pellets for added smoke flavor.

4. Arrange the chicken on the grill, close the lid, and smoke for 1 hour to 1 hour 30 minutes, or until a meat thermometer inserted in the thickest part of the thigh reads 165°F.

5. Let the meat rest for 5 minutes and baste with the reserved jerk paste prior to serving.

Pair It   Round out your menu with Roasted Okra (page 151).

SMO-FRIED CHICKEN

Serves 4 to 6

PREP TIME: 30 MINUTES

SMOKE TIME: 55 MINUTES

 SMOKE TEMPERATURE: 375°F, 325°F

 WOOD PELLETS: PECAN OR ALDER

1 egg, beaten

½ cup milk

1 cup all-purpose flour

2 tablespoons salt

1 tablespoon freshly ground black pepper

2 teaspoons freshly ground white pepper

2 teaspoons cayenne pepper

2 teaspoons garlic powder

2 teaspoons onion powder

1 teaspoon smoked paprika

8 tablespoons (1 stick) unsalted butter, melted

1 whole chicken, cut up into pieces

I have never been able to master fried chicken at home. Pan-frying, deep-frying, and even using the Instant Pot wouldn't work for me. I always ended up with a funky texture—and a slippery floor. Enter the wood pellet grill. I use only five herbs and spices, but with the addition of *smoke*, even the Colonel would deem this finger-lickin' good! You'll need your grill's higher temperature to produce the crunchy "fried" skin. The flavor and crunch end up better on the grill, and your kitchen will remain cool and clean in the process.

1. Supply your smoker with wood pellets and follow the manufacturer's specific start-up procedure. Preheat, with the lid closed, to 375°F.

2. In a medium bowl, combine the beaten egg with the milk and set aside.

3. In a separate medium bowl, stir together the flour, salt, black pepper, white pepper, cayenne, garlic powder, onion powder, and smoked paprika.

4. Line the bottom and sides of a high-sided metal baking pan with aluminum foil to ease cleanup.

5. Pour the melted butter into the prepared pan.

6. Dip the chicken pieces one at a time in the egg mixture, and then coat well with the seasoned flour. Transfer to the baking pan.

7. Smoke the chicken in the pan of butter ("smo-fry") on the grill, with the lid closed, for 25 minutes, then reduce the heat to 325°F and turn the chicken pieces over.

8. Continue smoking with the lid closed for about 30 minutes, or until a meat thermometer inserted in the thickest part of each chicken piece reads 165°F.

9. Serve immediately.

Ingredient Tip Whole chickens are often cheaper than individual parts, especially when you're buying organic. Save a few bucks by learning how to quickly break the bird down yourself.

WOOD-SMOKED WHOLE TURKEY

Serves 6 to 8

PREP TIME: 10 MINUTES

SMOKE TIME: 5 TO 6 HOURS

 SMOKE
TEMPERATURE:
250°F

 WOOD PELLETS:
APPLE OR APPLE
MASH BLEND

1 (10- to 12-pound) turkey,
giblets removed

Extra-virgin olive oil,
for rubbing

¼ cup poultry seasoning

8 tablespoons (1 stick) unsalted
butter, melted

½ cup apple juice

2 teaspoons dried sage

2 teaspoons dried thyme

When I smell applewood smoke I automatically think of roast turkey. Well . . . that and bacon at a Cracker Barrel restaurant. Turkey has never been easier to cook than on a wood pellet grill. Just remember to rub a bit of the poultry seasoning under the skin and into the muscle. Seasoning will not penetrate thick turkey skin from the outside in.

1. Supply your smoker with wood pellets and follow the manufacturer's specific start-up procedure. Preheat, with the lid closed, to 250°F.

2. Rub the turkey with oil and season with the poultry seasoning inside and out, getting under the skin.

3. In a bowl, combine the melted butter, apple juice, sage, and thyme to use for basting.

4. Put the turkey in a roasting pan, place on the grill, close the lid, and grill for 5 to 6 hours, basting every hour, until the skin is brown and crispy, or until a meat thermometer inserted in the thickest part of the thigh reads 165°F.

5. Let the bird rest for 15 to 20 minutes before carving.

Ingredient Tip Salt is a preservative, so the shelf life of salted butter is longer than unsalted; however, I don't recommend using them interchangeably. I use unsalted butter in most recipes to control the amount of salt being added. If you use salted butter, make sure you taste as you go. It does make a difference.

SMOKED AIRLINE CHICKEN

Serves 2

MARINATING TIME: 4 HOURS

PREP TIME: 20 MINUTES

SMOKE TIME: 1 HOUR 30 MINUTES
TO 2 HOURS

 SMOKE
TEMPERATURE:
250°F

 WOOD PELLETS:
PECAN OR OAK

2 boneless chicken breasts
with drumettes attached

½ cup soy sauce

½ cup teriyaki sauce

¼ cup canola oil

¼ cup white vinegar

1 tablespoon minced garlic

¼ cup chopped scallions

2 teaspoons freshly ground
black pepper

1 teaspoon ground mustard

You may not have heard, but the airline chicken is going extinct. No, it's not a breed of bird; it's a now rarely seen cut of chicken. Sometimes called "Statler chicken," "hotel cut," or a "frenched breast," it is a skin-on, boneless chicken breast with the first segment of the wing, or drumette, still attached. It's a relic of the days when many flights offered "fancy" hot meals. You never find this cut in the grocery store, so you'll need to trim your own from a whole bird or have a butcher do it for you. I prefer white meat over dark, so this combines my favorite parts of the chicken. Plus, the pellet smoke adds incredible flavor that the airlines could never achieve.

1. Place the chicken in a baking dish.

2. In a bowl, whisk together the soy sauce, teriyaki sauce, canola oil, vinegar, garlic, scallions, pepper and ground mustard, then pour this marinade over the chicken, coating both sides.

3. Refrigerate the chicken in marinade for 4 hours, turning over every hour.

4. When ready to smoke the chicken, supply your smoker with wood pellets and follow the manufacturer's specific start-up procedure. Preheat, with the lid closed, to 250°F.

5. Remove the chicken from the marinade but do not rinse. Discard the marinade.

6. Arrange the chicken directly on the grill, close the lid, and smoke for 1 hour 30 minutes to 2 hours, or until a meat thermometer inserted in the thickest part of the meat reads 165°F.

7. Let the meat rest for 3 minutes before serving.

Pair It **Pair this dish with Brussels Sprout Bites with Cilantro-Balsamic Drizzle (page 155).**

TRADITIONAL BBQ CHICKEN

Serves 8

PREP TIME: 10 MINUTES

SMOKE TIME: 1 HOUR 30 MINUTES
TO 2 HOURS

 SMOKE
TEMPERATURE:
250°F

 WOOD PELLETS:
MAPLE OR CHERRY

8 boneless, skinless
chicken breasts

2 teaspoons salt

2 teaspoons freshly ground
black pepper

2 teaspoons garlic powder

2 cups Bill's Best BBQ Sauce
(page 183) or your preferred
barbecue sauce, divided

A simple moist chicken breast with smoke flavor is something
wood pellet grills do very well. I recommend taking it low and
slow to allow the white meat to absorb as much smoke as
possible. However, if you are in a hurry, you can boost the cook
temperature to 350°F and cut the cook time down to 30 minutes.
Note: I suggest using a sweet wood pellet flavor in this recipe to
complement the barbecue sauce.

1. Supply your smoker with wood pellets and follow the manufacturer's
   specific start-up procedure. Preheat, with the lid closed, to 250°F.

2. Place the chicken breasts in a large pan and sprinkle both sides with the
   salt, pepper, and garlic powder, being sure to rub under the skin.

3. Place the roasting pan on the grill, close the lid, and smoke for 1 hour
   30 minutes to 2 hours, or until a meat thermometer inserted in the
   thickest part of each breast reads 165°F. During the last 15 minutes of
   cooking, cover the chicken with 1 cup of barbecue sauce.

4. Serve the chicken warm with the remaining 1 cup of barbecue sauce.

Pair It Serve with Mexican Street Corn with Chipotle Butter
(page 149).

WILD WEST WINGS

Serves 4

PREP TIME: 10 MINUTES

SMOKE TIME: 50 TO 60 MINUTES

 SMOKE
TEMPERATURE:
350°F

 WOOD PELLETS:
OAK

2 pounds chicken wings

2 tablespoons extra-virgin
olive oil

2 packages ranch dressing mix
(such as Hidden Valley brand)

¼ cup prepared ranch dressing
(optional)

Wood pellet smokers are a secret weapon for preparing wings on the grill. On typical grills, fatty drippings inevitably cause massive flareups and grease fires. Not so with pellet power. The indirect heat and large drip pan protects against flareups. Salt, pepper, and smoke alone are enough to make wings delicious, but if you like to experiment, try this zesty ranch rub instead. For a double dose of ranch, you can serve these wings with ranch dressing as a dipping sauce.

1. Supply your smoker with wood pellets and follow the manufacturer's specific start-up procedure. Preheat, with the lid closed, to 350°F.

2. Place the chicken wings in a large bowl and toss with the olive oil and ranch dressing mix.

3. Arrange the wings directly on the grill, or line the grill with aluminum foil for easy cleanup, close the lid, and smoke for 25 minutes.

4. Flip and smoke for 20 to 35 minutes more, or until a meat thermometer inserted in the thickest part of the wings reads 165°F and the wings are crispy. (Note: The wings will likely be done after 45 minutes, but an extra 10 to 15 minutes makes them crispy without drying the meat.)

5. Serve warm with ranch dressing (if using).

Pair It **Kick up your menu by serving these wings with Bacon-Wrapped Jalapeño Poppers (page 163).**

Chapter 4
PORK

Unless you're in Texas, most people think of pork when they think of barbecue. The "other white meat" is chock-full of marbled fat and succulence, and the sweet meat (still technically considered red meat) absorbs smoke wonderfully. Pork barbecue has a long and storied history. Christopher Columbus noted in his writings that the Taíno people of the Caribbean cooked in a style featuring a grid of green sticks over indirect campfire heat that they deemed "barbacoa." According to barbecue historians (I want that job!), it was near Santa Elena, South Carolina (modern-day Parris Island, near Beaufort and Hilton Head Island), that the Spanish and American Indians forged barbecue history around a flickering campfire. As it turns out, I make my home in nearby Charleston, and I can say from experience that barbecue in the South is most certainly about perfecting all parts of the humble pig. ◊

◀ PICKLED-PEPPER PORK CHOPS, page 78, with SWEET AND SPICY JALAPEÑO RELISH, page 192

CUTS

There's no barbecue feast quite as fine as one that includes a whole hog. Although there are competition-size trailer-bound wood pellet smokers, most of the ones sold these days can only handle smaller cuts. Pork shoulder remains the slow-smoking leader in the South. In fact, to many Southerners, barbecue is synonymous with pulled or chopped smoked pork butt. You should also know that the butt is really the shoulder of the pig, and the rear or hindquarter is the ham. Wood pellet grills are often built to resemble large offset smokers and can usually accommodate any individual cut from the massive whole shoulder to the pork belly, hams, and ribs. After you run through all of those big cuts, there's still plenty of pork to work with, from sausage to tenderloin. Some of my favorite selections, like rib tips and cracklings, are sometimes considered scraps!

TECHNIQUES

There are dozens of ways to prepare pork. From going big with a whole hog to curing bacon, the task can be as big or as small as your imagination desires. I love the way a spicy brine saturates a good pork chop. If you have a large roast, you can rub it, inject it, and later wrap it in aluminum foil. One ultimate goal for roasts and ribs is to build a beautiful bark. The dark-brown crust can be enhanced by steady smoke, the right rub, intermittent basting, and layering sauce over the course of the cook.

When it comes to a Boston butt, the technique of pulling apart the softened meat fibers into long strands is known as "pulled pork." Pulled pork is usually comprised of a small pork shoulder, but if you are serving a group, one technique for increasing the amount of lean white meat is to mix in the meat of an uncured whole ham or pork loin.

The big trick to pulled pork is that you'll need to achieve higher internal temperatures to achieve that pull-apart texture. Sure, the USDA says it's "done" when you hit 160°F, but in order to break down the collagen and intramuscular fat in a big pork roast, you need to top 200°F. It is only then that your temperature probe will slide into the meat with little to no resistance. Serving on a bun or white bread is optional.

If you're looking for a technique to produce fall-off-the-bone ribs, simply remember the 3-2-1 method: Smoke your ribs for 3 hours, wrap them in foil and cook for 2 more hours, and then smoke them unwrapped for 1 hour to firm up the bark. It's a long process, but good things come to those who wait.

Finally, one of the most popular techniques for making spare ribs is to neatly trim them "St. Louis–style," a term for a full rack of spare ribs that is shaped into a tidy elongated rectangle. This makes for a nice presentation, but there's nothing wrong with that meat you may have trimmed off in the process. It has a name, too: rib tips. You can cook the rib tips along with the full slabs to help track cooking.

RULES TO GRILL BY

Pork barbecue is one of the most popular meats for low-and-slow smoking on a pellet smoker. Here are a few more tips to up your pork barbecue game:

★ The convection-like heating of wood pellet grills can benefit from a water pan. Nestle a pan filled with water or juice in a corner of your grill to add a bit of moisture to long cooks (as with ribs).

★ Pork chops edged with a succulent layer of fat tend to curl up during grilling. Avoid the curl by scoring the fatty rim with a few cuts.

★ Great flavor starts with high-quality meat. Consider antibiotic-free, heritage, and premium breeds, such as Kurobuta (I have a few sourced at www.BarbecueTricks.com/resources).

★ Better ribs start at the market. Look for meaty slabs, and avoid racks with spots of exposed bones, also known as "shiners."

★ Pulled pork and ribs need to hit internal temperatures that are much higher than USDA recommendations. Target 205°F for butts to achieve pull-apart tenderness. Invest in a quality instant-read electric meat thermometer.

★ You'll want to remove the tough membrane on the back side of pork ribs *before* cooking to allow for better smoke and spice penetration. Enlist the help of a sheet of paper towel to grip the membrane and give it a good hard tug to peel it off those ribs.

★ Pork ribs come with their own natural "pop-up" thermometer. Look for the ends of the bones to extrude from the meat as a telltale sign of doneness.

BABY BACK RIBS

Serves 4

PREP TIME: 15 MINUTES

SMOKE TIME: 5 HOURS 30 MINUTES
TO 6 HOURS

 SMOKE
TEMPERATURE:
150° TO 180°F
("SMOKE"), 225°F

 WOOD PELLETS:
HICKORY OR
COMPETITION BLEND

2 full slabs baby back ribs, back
membranes removed

1 cup prepared table mustard

1 cup Our House Dry Rub
(page 190)

1 cup apple juice, divided

1 cup packed light brown
sugar, divided

1 cup Bill's Best BBQ Sauce
(page 183), divided

I used to claim baby backs as my favorite food of all time. Having grown up near Chicago, I remember slabs that were generally thin with delicious meat, but that had long, spindly bones. The flesh was very white and clean, and it was always heavily glazed with sauce. It's true that baby back ribs are different from spare ribs, in that they come from the top of the rib cage and not the bottom near the belly like spares. But these days, I just can't seem to find the same characteristics I remember from my youth in grocery store baby backs. I'm now convinced it is more *the source and breed of pig* that make the difference. The good news is that there's new interest in heritage breeds and meat sourcing. I'm on an Internet hunt to find a rib match for my memory. If you find 'em first, e-mail me: Bill@BarbecueTricks.com!

1. Supply your smoker with wood pellets and follow the manufacturer's specific start-up procedure. Preheat, with the lid closed, to 150° to 180°F, or to the "Smoke" setting.

2. Coat the ribs with the mustard to help the rub stick and lock in moisture.

3. Generously apply the rub.

4. Place the ribs directly on the grill, close the lid, and smoke for 3 hours.

5. Increase the temperature to 225°F.

6. Remove the ribs from the grill and wrap each rack individually with aluminum foil, but before sealing tightly, add ½ cup apple juice and ½ cup brown sugar to each package.

7. Return the foil-wrapped ribs to the grill, close the lid, and smoke for 2 more hours.

8. Carefully unwrap the ribs and remove the foil completely. Coat each slab with ½ cup of barbecue sauce and continue smoking with the lid closed for 30 minutes to 1 hour, or until the meat tightens and has a reddish bark. For the perfect rack, the internal temperature should be 190°F.

Smoking Tip Instant-read digital thermometers are a must for outdoor cooking, but using the thermometer on ribs can be tricky. To get an accurate reading, avoid probing too close to the bones. An easy trick is to use a toothpick to probe ½ inch into the meat between the ends of two bones. If the toothpick slides in with very little resistance, the ribs are ready to serve.

NOT YO' TYPICAL NACHOS

Serves 4

PREP TIME: 15 MINUTES

SMOKE TIME: 10 MINUTES

 SMOKE
TEMPERATURE:
375°F

 WOOD PELLETS:
MESQUITE OR
HICKORY

2 cups leftover smoked
pulled pork

1 small sweet onion, diced

1 medium tomato, diced

1 jalapeño pepper, seeded
and diced

1 garlic clove, minced

1 teaspoon salt

1 teaspoon freshly ground
black pepper

1 bag tortilla chips

1 cup shredded
Cheddar cheese

½ cup Bill's Best BBQ Sauce
(page 183), divided

½ cup shredded jalapeño
Monterey Jack cheese

Juice of ½ lime

1 avocado, halved, pitted,
and sliced

2 tablespoons sour cream

1 tablespoon chopped fresh
cilantro

If you smoke a lot of Boston butts, chances are you will have leftover pulled pork from time to time. I like to utilize the extra pork to top everything from loaded baked potatoes to pizza and more. However, my family's favorite quick fix is this nacho dish. Everything is already cooked, so all you need to do is heat it up and melt the cheese.

1. Supply your smoker with wood pellets and follow the manufacturer's specific start-up procedure. Preheat, with the lid closed, to 375°F.

2. Heat the pulled pork in the microwave.

3. In a medium bowl, combine the onion, tomato, jalapeño, garlic, salt, and pepper, and set aside.

4. Arrange half of the tortilla chips in a large cast iron skillet. Spread half of the warmed pork on top and cover with the Cheddar cheese. Top with half of the onion-jalapeño mixture, then drizzle with ¼ cup of barbecue sauce.

5. Layer on the remaining tortilla chips, then the remaining pork and the Monterey Jack cheese. Top with the remaining onion-jalapeño mixture and drizzle with the remaining ¼ cup of barbecue sauce.

6. Place the skillet on the grill, close the lid, and smoke for about 10 minutes, or until the cheese is melted and bubbly. (Watch to make sure your chips don't burn!)

7. Squeeze the lime juice over the nachos, top with the avocado slices and sour cream, and garnish with the cilantro before serving hot.

Smoking Tip A large cast iron skillet is not only a great cooking vessel for the grill, but it is also an impressive, heat-retaining serving platter. Just invest in a handle hot pad to keep from burning yourself.

BBQ BREAKFAST GRITS

Serves 8

PREP TIME: 20 MINUTES

SMOKE TIME: 30 TO 40 MINUTES

 SMOKE
TEMPERATURE:
350°F

 WOOD PELLETS:
HICKORY

2 cups chicken stock

1 cup water

1 cup quick-cooking grits

3 tablespoons unsalted butter

2 tablespoons minced garlic

1 medium onion, chopped

1 jalapeño pepper, stemmed,
seeded, and chopped

1 teaspoon cayenne pepper

2 teaspoons red pepper flakes

1 tablespoon hot sauce

1 cup shredded Monterey
Jack cheese

1 cup sour cream

Salt

Freshly ground black pepper

2 eggs, beaten

⅓ cup half-and-half

3 cups leftover pulled pork
(preferably smoked)

Finally barbecue has made its way to the breakfast table. This is another opportunity to get creative with leftover pulled pork. Smoked pulled pork freezes well, and so does this casserole. Pull it out when you have company, and they'll be impressed.

1. Supply your smoker with wood pellets and follow the manufacturer's specific start-up procedure. Preheat, with the lid closed, to 350°F.

2. On your kitchen stovetop, in a large saucepan over high heat, bring the chicken stock and water to a boil.

3. Add the grits and reduce the heat to low, then stir in the butter, garlic, onion, jalapeño, cayenne, red pepper flakes, hot sauce, cheese, and sour cream. Season with salt and pepper, then cook for about 5 minutes.

4. Temper the beaten eggs (see Tip below) and incorporate into the grits. Remove the saucepan from the heat and stir in the half-and-half and pulled pork.

5. Pour the grits into a greased grill-safe 9-by-13-inch casserole dish or aluminum pan.

6. Transfer to the grill, close the lid, and bake for 30 to 40 minutes, covering with aluminum foil toward the end of cooking if the grits start to get too brown on top.

Ingredient Tip Tempering eggs is a technique for adding them to already hot ingredients without ending up with scrambled eggs. The trick is to combine things slowly. Beat your eggs in a separate bowl and slowly bring up their temperature by mixing in small amounts of slightly cooled grits mixture until you can finally add them to the saucepan.

CANDIED SPARERIBS

Serves 4 to 5

PREP TIME: 10 MINUTES

SMOKE TIME: 6 HOURS

 SMOKE
TEMPERATURE:
250°F

 WOOD PELLETS:
MESQUITE OR CHERRY

2 racks pork spareribs, membrane removed from back

2 tablespoons yellow mustard

2 tablespoons chicken bouillon granules

1 tablespoon red pepper flakes

¼ cup apple juice, divided

1 cup Blueberry BBQ Sauce (page 191), plus more for serving

Competition-worthy spareribs feature meat that comes loose with a gentle tug, leaving behind a bare (almost white) bone peeking through a perfect half-moon–shaped bite. But most people like a fall-off-the-bone rib, where it's smoked to succulence. The method to achieve this is as easy as 3-2-1. The trick is to break down the low-and-slow cooking process into three easy-to-remember segments, including some time for the ribs to smoke wrapped in foil (see the full explanation on page 62). The "3-2-1" trick works effortlessly on pellet smokers.

1. Supply your smoker with wood pellets and follow the manufacturer's specific start-up procedure. Preheat, with the lid closed, to 250°F.

2. Coat the ribs with the mustard, then sprinkle the ribs on all sides with the bouillon granules and red pepper flakes.

3. Place the ribs directly on the grill, close the lid, and smoke for 3 hours.

4. Remove the ribs from the grill and wrap each rack individually with aluminum foil, but before sealing tightly, add 2 tablespoons of apple juice to each package.

5. Place the foil-wrapped ribs back on the grill, close the lid, and continue smoking for 2 hours.

6. Carefully unwrap the ribs and remove the foil completely. Baste the ribs with the barbecue sauce, then smoke with the lid closed for 1 hour more.

7. Let the ribs rest for about 5 minutes before serving with additional barbecue sauce.

Ingredient Tip Before seasoning the ribs, you'll want to remove that tough membrane on the inside because it inhibits smoke and spice from permeating the meat. It's easy to remove: Use a butter knife to pick loose one corner of the membrane, then use a dry paper towel to grasp and carefully peel off the remainder of the tough tissue.

LIP-SMACKIN' PORK LOIN

Serves 8

PREP TIME: 10 MINUTES

SMOKE TIME: 3 HOURS

 SMOKE
TEMPERATURE:
250°F

 WOOD PELLETS:
APPLE OR HICKORY

¼ cup finely ground coffee

¼ cup paprika

¼ cup garlic powder

2 tablespoons chili powder

1 tablespoon packed light
brown sugar

1 tablespoon ground allspice

1 tablespoon ground coriander

1 tablespoon freshly ground
black pepper

2 teaspoons ground mustard

1½ teaspoons celery seeds

1 (1½- to 2-pound) pork
loin roast

The pork loin differs a bit from the pricier, smaller, and more tender pork tenderloin, but both cuts cook nicely on a wood pellet grill thanks to the grill's steady and dependable low temperature. It used to be that most pork got overcooked due to a fear of trichinosis, but these days, that disease is extremely rare. Plus, trichinae (the parasites that cause it) are killed at 137°F. Pork loin and pork tenderloin can now safely be served rare and are great sources of lean, healthy protein.

1. Supply your smoker with wood pellets and follow the manufacturer's specific start-up procedure. Preheat, with the lid closed, to 250°F.

2. In a small bowl, combine the ground coffee, paprika, garlic powder, chili powder, brown sugar, allspice, coriander, pepper, mustard, and celery seeds to create a rub, and generously apply it to the pork loin roast.

3. Place the pork loin on the grill, fat-side up, close the lid, and roast for 3 hours, or until a meat thermometer inserted in the thickest part of the meat reads 160°F.

4. Let the pork rest for 5 minutes before slicing and serving.

Pair It Try serving this pork loin with the Georgia Sweet Onion Bake (page 157).

PIG POPS (SWEET-HOT BACON ON A STICK)

Makes 24

PREP TIME: 15 MINUTES
SMOKE TIME: 25 TO 30 MINUTES

 SMOKE
TEMPERATURE:
350°F

 WOOD PELLETS:
HICKORY OR MAPLE

Nonstick cooking spray, oil, or butter, for greasing

2 pounds thick-cut bacon (24 slices)

24 metal skewers

1 cup packed light brown sugar

2 to 3 teaspoons cayenne pepper

½ cup maple syrup, divided

You'll never forget your first bite of candied bacon. It almost always results in a response like, "Where has this been all my life?" In fact, bacon is notoriously hard to cook on a normal grill because the slices can fall through the grate and there are flareups. Using your wood pellet grill and skewers, a baking sheet, or a Frogmat will make it much easier. Note: For crispier bacon, smoke at 350°F for 25 to 30 minutes.

1. Supply your smoker with wood pellets and follow the manufacturer's specific start-up procedure. Preheat, with the lid closed, to 350°F.

2. Coat a disposable aluminum foil baking sheet with cooking spray, oil, or butter.

3. Thread each bacon slice onto a metal skewer and place on the prepared baking sheet.

4. In a medium bowl, stir together the brown sugar and cayenne.

5. Baste the top sides of the bacon with ¼ cup of maple syrup.

6. Sprinkle half of the brown sugar mixture over the bacon.

7. Place the baking sheet on the grill, close the lid, and smoke for 15 to 30 minutes.

8. Using tongs, flip the bacon skewers. Baste with the remaining ¼ cup of maple syrup and top with the remaining brown sugar mixture.

9. Continue smoking with the lid closed for 10 to 15 minutes, or until crispy. You can eyeball the bacon and smoke to your desired doneness, but the actual ideal internal temperature for bacon is 155°F (if you want to try to get a thermometer into it—ha!).

10. Using tongs, carefully remove the bacon skewers from the grill. Let cool completely before handling.

Smoking Tip If you'd prefer to use wooden skewers, soak them in water for 30 minutes before threading on the bacon.

PINEAPPLE-PEPPER PORK KEBABS

Serves 6

MARINATING TIME: 1 TO 4 HOURS
PREP TIME: 20 MINUTES
SMOKE TIME: 10 TO 12 MINUTES

 SMOKE
TEMPERATURE:
450°F

 WOOD PELLETS:
APPLE OR CHERRY

1 (20-ounce) bottle
hoisin sauce

½ cup Sriracha

¼ cup honey

¼ cup apple cider vinegar

2 tablespoons canola oil

2 teaspoons minced garlic

2 teaspoons onion powder

1 teaspoon ground ginger

1 teaspoon salt

1 teaspoon freshly ground
black pepper

2 pounds thick-cut pork
chops or pork loin, cut into
2-inch cubes

10 ounces fresh pineapple, cut
into chunks

1 red onion, cut into wedges

1 bag mini sweet peppers, tops
removed and seeded

12 metal or wooden skewers
(soaked in water for 30 minutes
if wooden)

If the only meat on a stick you've ever tried is a corn dog, it's time I broaden your horizons. Kebabs are an easy way to mix different flavors on the grill, and they've been around for a long time. The first known use of the word "kebab" was in 1377; it is widely thought to have originated in Turkey.

1. In a small bowl, stir together the hoisin, Sriracha, honey, vinegar, oil, minced garlic, onion powder, ginger, salt, and black pepper to create the marinade. Reserve ¼ cup for basting.

2. Toss the pork cubes, pineapple chunks, onion wedges, and mini peppers in the remaining marinade. Cover and refrigerate for at least 1 hour or up to 4 hours.

3. Supply your smoker with wood pellets and follow the manufacturer's specific start-up procedure. Preheat, with the lid closed, to 450°F.

4. Remove the pork, pineapple, and veggies from the marinade; do not rinse. Discard the marinade.

5. Use the double-skewer technique to assemble the kebabs (see Tip below). Thread each of 6 skewers with a piece of pork, a piece of pineapple, a piece of onion, and a sweet mini pepper, making sure that the skewer goes through the left side of the ingredients. Repeat the threading on each skewer two more times. Double-skewer the kebabs by sticking another 6 skewers through the right side of the ingredients.

6. Place the kebabs directly on the grill, close the lid, and smoke for 10 to 12 minutes, turning once. They are done when a meat thermometer inserted in the pork reads 160°F.

Smoking Tip **Double-skewering your kebabs keeps the meat from spinning on the grill and allows for better overall maneuverability.**

SIMPLE CREAM CHEESE SAUSAGE BALLS

Serves 4 to 5

PREP TIME: 15 MINUTES

SMOKE TIME: 30 MINUTES

 SMOKE
TEMPERATURE:
350°F

 WOOD PELLETS:
HICKORY

1 pound ground hot sausage, uncooked

8 ounces cream cheese, softened

1 package mini filo dough shells

Though they can be hard to find, mini filo dough shells are very versatile appetizer bases. So when you *do* find them, stock up. They freeze well, and the possibilities are endless for time-saving hors d'oeuvres. Plus, because your pellet smoker can maintain baking temperatures, they are now welcome at the grill. Canned biscuits divided in half or wonton wrappers also work in a pinch.

1. Supply your smoker with wood pellets and follow the manufacturer's specific start-up procedure. Preheat, with the lid closed, to 350°F.

2. In a large bowl, using your hands, thoroughly mix together the sausage and cream cheese until well blended.

3. Place the filo dough shells on a rimmed perforated pizza pan or into a mini muffin tin.

4. Roll the sausage and cheese mixture into 1-inch balls and place into the filo shells.

5. Place the pizza pan or mini muffin tin on the grill, close the lid, and smoke the sausage balls for 30 minutes, or until cooked through and the sausage is no longer pink.

6. Plate and serve warm.

Pair It Serve these along with Not Yo' Typical Nachos (page 65) and you've got game day covered!

PARTY PULLED PORK SHOULDER

Serves 10

PREP TIME: 30 MINUTES

SMOKE TIME: 8 TO 9 HOURS

 SMOKE
TEMPERATURE:
225°F

 WOOD PELLETS:
HICKORY AND
CHARCOAL BLEND

1 (5-pound) Boston butt (pork shoulder)

¼ cup prepared table mustard

½ cup Our House Dry Rub (page 190) or your favorite rub, divided

2 cups apple juice

½ cup salt

Bill's Best BBQ Sauce (page 183), for serving

One of the barbecue world's most popular cuts of meat is the Boston butt. Now, you need to know that the butt isn't the actual butt of the pork. The butt is the shoulder. Got it? Somewhere along the way, butchers stored and transported these cuts in barrels called "butts," thus the name. The Boston butt, picnic shoulder, and whole shoulder can all be used here, but you'll need to account for a lot more time for a lot more weight.

1. Slather the meat with the mustard and coat with ¼ cup of the dry rub.

2. In a spray bottle, mix together the apple juice and salt and shake until the salt is dissolved.

3. Supply your smoker with wood pellets and follow the manufacturer's specific start-up procedure. Preheat, with the lid closed, to 225°F.

4. Place the pork fat-side up in an aluminum pan, transfer to the grill, close the lid, and smoke for 8 to 9 hours, spritzing well all over with the salted apple juice every hour, until a meat thermometer inserted in the thickest part of the meat reads 205°F. Cover the pork loosely with aluminum foil toward the end of cooking, if necessary, to keep the top from blackening.

5. Drain the liquid from the pan, cover, and allow the meat to cool for a few minutes before using two forks to shred it.

6. Sprinkle the remaining rub over the meat and serve with barbecue sauce.

Smoking Tip USDA standard for "done" may be food-safe, but it isn't enough to break down the collagen and fats to get your pork to fork-tender pit master standards. You need to get the internal temperature higher than 200°F to achieve pull-apart succulence. General rule of thumb: If the pork does not pull apart easily with two forks, it's not ready. Think fall-off-the-bone.

SCOTCH EGGS

Serves 4 to 6

CHILL TIME: 2 HOURS
PREP TIME: 30 MINUTES
SMOKE TIME: 1 HOUR 30 MINUTES

 SMOKE
TEMPERATURE:
150° TO 180°F
("SMOKE"), 375°F

 WOOD PELLETS:
HICKORY

½ cup all-purpose flour

4 teaspoons poultry
seasoning, divided

4 hard-boiled eggs, peeled

1 pound ground hot sausage

1 egg, beaten

1 cup panko breadcrumbs

1 cup mayonnaise

¼ cup Dijon mustard

Scotch eggs and armadillo eggs are both popular items to explore on pellet smokers. The recipe here consists of sausage-wrapped hard-boiled eggs, and it originated in the UK. Armadillo eggs are all-American and contain no eggs (and no armadillo). They are simply cheese-stuffed jalapeños wrapped with sausage and bacon. If you're bold, you may want to try dragon eggs, which are sausage-wrapped like the others, but brace yourself for a habanero center.

1. In a small bowl, combine the flour and 2 teaspoons of poultry seasoning.

2. Dip the hard-boiled eggs in water, then roll them around in the flour mixture.

3. Divide the sausage into four equal parts and roll into balls.

4. Flatten the balls and shape them around the hard-boiled eggs until completely covered.

5. Dip each sausage-covered egg in the beaten egg, then dredge in the panko. Transfer to a plate, loosely cover with plastic wrap, and refrigerate for 2 hours.

6. In a bowl, whisk together the mayonnaise, mustard, and remaining 2 teaspoons of poultry seasoning to create a dipping sauce. Set aside.

7. Supply your smoker with wood pellets and follow the manufacturer's specific start-up procedure. Preheat, with the lid closed, to 150° to 180°F, or to the "Smoke" setting.

8. Put the chilled eggs directly on the grill, close the lid, and smoke for 1 hour. Remove from the grill.

9. Increase the temperature to 375°F and return the eggs to the grill. Close the lid and smoke for 30 more minutes.

10. Let the eggs cool for 5 minutes before slicing and serving with the dipping sauce.

Pair It Pair the smoked eggs with the cool crunch of Broccoli-Cauliflower Salad (page 153).

JALAPEÑO-BACON PORK TENDERLOIN

Serves 4 to 6

PREP TIME: 25 MINUTES

SMOKE TIME: 2 HOURS 30 MINUTES

 SMOKE
TEMPERATURE:
225°F, 375°F

 WOOD PELLETS:
HICKORY OR APPLE

¼ cup yellow mustard

2 (1-pound) pork tenderloins

¼ cup Our House Dry Rub
(page 190)

8 ounces cream cheese,
softened

1 cup grated Cheddar cheese

1 tablespoon unsalted
butter, melted

1 tablespoon minced garlic

2 jalapeño peppers, seeded
and diced

1½ pounds bacon

The pork loin and the pork tenderloin are both fantastic meats for absorbing smoke flavors on the grill. But did you know they are really separate cuts from different parts of the hog? The tenderloin is quite a bit smaller than the loin, which is often covered in a layer of fat. Tenderloins may have a bit of silverskin to remove but are otherwise lean and delicious. For this dish, the pork can be served on the rare side and pink in the center.

1. Slather the mustard all over the pork tenderloins, then sprinkle generously with the dry rub to coat the meat.

2. Supply your smoker with wood pellets and follow the manufacturer's specific start-up procedure. Preheat, with the lid closed, to 225°F.

3. Place the tenderloins directly on the grill, close the lid, and smoke for 2 hours.

4. Remove the pork from the grill and increase the temperature to 375°F.

5. In a small bowl, combine the cream cheese, Cheddar cheese, melted butter, garlic, and jalapeños.

6. Starting from the top, slice deeply along the center of each tenderloin end to end, creating a cavity.

7. Spread half of the cream cheese mixture in the cavity of one tenderloin. Repeat with the remaining mixture and the other piece of meat.

8. Securely wrap one tenderloin with half of the bacon. Repeat with the remaining bacon and the other piece of meat.

9. Transfer the bacon-wrapped tenderloins to the grill, close the lid, and smoke for about 30 minutes, or until a meat thermometer inserted in the thickest part of the meat reads 160°F and the bacon is browned and cooked through.

10. Let the tenderloins rest for 5 to 10 minutes before slicing and serving.

Technique Tip A bacon wrap adds a nice amount of self-basting fat to the lean tenderloin in this recipe. If you want to amp up the table conversation, try encasing the pork with a bacon *weave*. It's double the bacon, and double the fun. Start with a flat surface and 8 cold strips of bacon lying close together vertically. Then weave 8 more strips horizontally under and over the vertical strips. It takes a few tries to get right, but it looks amazing. You can hide ragged edges in the seam on the bottom of the small roast.

SMOKED BRATS

Serves 10

PREP TIME: 10 MINUTES

SMOKE TIME: 1 HOUR 30 MINUTES
TO 2 HOURS

 SMOKE
TEMPERATURE:
225°F

 WOOD PELLETS:
OAK OR PECAN

4 (12-ounce) cans of beer

2 onions, sliced into rings

2 green bell peppers, sliced
into rings

2 tablespoons unsalted butter,
plus more for the rolls

2 tablespoons red
pepper flakes

10 brats, uncooked

10 hoagie rolls, split

Mustard, for serving

In the United States, brats have become a football tailgate staple. But bratwurst is actually an old German name. Derived from *brät*, which is finely chopped meat, and *wurst*, which means sausage, brats are almost like fine cheese in that there are so many different varieties. The main thing to keep in mind is that the inside of a fresh brat is raw, unlike a hot dog that is always precooked. You'll want to use an instant-read meat thermometer to confirm that you're hitting an internal temperature of 160°F.

1. On your kitchen stovetop, in a large saucepan over high heat, bring the beer, onions, peppers, butter, and red pepper flakes to a boil.

2. Supply your smoker with wood pellets and follow the manufacturer's specific start-up procedure. Preheat, with the lid closed, to 225°F.

3. Place a disposable pan on one side of grill, and pour the warmed beer mixture into it, creating a "brat tub" (see Tip below).

4. Place the brats on the other side of the grill, directly on the grate, and close the lid and smoke for 1 hour, turning 2 or 3 times.

5. Add the brats to the pan with the onions and peppers, cover tightly with aluminum foil, and continue smoking with the lid closed for 30 minutes to 1 hour, or until a meat thermometer inserted in the brats reads 160°F.

6. Butter the cut sides of the hoagie rolls and toast cut-side down on the grill.

7. Using a slotted spoon, remove the brats, onions, and peppers from the cooking liquid and discard the liquid.

8. Serve the brats on the toasted buns, topped with the onions and peppers and mustard (ketchup optional).

Smoking Tip When grilling brats for a crowd, have a "brat tub" on the grill to act as a holding tank once your sausages are cooked. This will allow you to keep the pellet grill running without burning your brats, and the sliced onions and green bell peppers can also be used as toppings.

COUNTRY PORK ROAST

Serves 8

PREP TIME: 20 MINUTES

SMOKE TIME: 3 HOURS

 SMOKE
TEMPERATURE:
250°F

 WOOD PELLETS:
APPLE OR HICKORY

1 (28-ounce) jar or 2
(14.5-ounce) cans sauerkraut

3 Granny Smith apples, cored
and chopped

¾ cup packed light
brown sugar

3 tablespoons Greek seasoning

2 teaspoons dried basil leaves

Extra-virgin olive oil,
for rubbing

1 (2- to 2½-pound) pork
loin roast

The pork loin roast is one of my favorite cuts of the pig because, like a blank canvas, there are a lot of ways to prepare it. You can even add it to pulled Boston butt to increase the white meat mix. And the loin is nice and lean, a good choice if you are watching your waistline. I really should be doing that. . . .

1. Supply your smoker with wood pellets and follow the manufacturer's specific start-up procedure. Preheat, with the lid closed, to 250°F.

2. In a large bowl, stir together the sauerkraut, chopped apples, and brown sugar.

3. Spread the sauerkraut-apple mixture in the bottom of a 9-by-13-inch baking dish.

4. In a small bowl, mix together the Greek seasoning and dried basil for the rub.

5. Oil the pork roast and apply the rub, then place it fat-side up in the baking dish, on top of the sauerkraut.

6. Transfer the baking dish to the grill, close the lid, and roast the pork for 3 hours, or until a meat thermometer inserted in the thickest part of the meat reads 160°F.

7. Remove the pork roast from the baking dish and let rest for 5 minutes before slicing.

8. To serve, divide the sauerkraut-apple mixture among plates and top with the sliced pork.

Pair It Make your meal a study in cabbage by pairing this pork roast with Southern Slaw (page 156).

PICKLED-PEPPER PORK CHOPS

Serves 4

MARINATING TIME: 4 HOURS
TO OVERNIGHT

PREP TIME: 15 MINUTES

SMOKE TIME: 45 TO 50 MINUTES

 SMOKE
TEMPERATURE:
325°F

 WOOD PELLETS:
OAK OR HICKORY

4 (1-inch-thick) pork chops

½ cup pickled jalapeño juice or
pickle juice

¼ cup chopped pickled (jarred)
jalapeño pepper slices

¼ cup chopped roasted
red peppers

¼ cup canned diced tomatoes,
well-drained

¼ cup chopped scallions

2 teaspoons poultry seasoning

2 teaspoons salt

2 teaspoons freshly ground
black pepper

I am a self-proclaimed chili head, and I burn through a lot of pickled jalapeños. This marinade is a result of me trying to show some resourcefulness. Use the zesty jalapeño juice to fire things up before the chops even touch the grill. You could use pickle juice instead for a low-heat option.

1. Pour the jalapeño juice into a large container with a lid. Add the pork chops, cover, and marinate in the refrigerator for at least 4 hours or overnight, supplementing with or substituting pickle juice as desired.

2. In a small bowl, combine the chopped pickled jalapeños, roasted red peppers, tomatoes, scallions, and poultry seasoning to make a relish. Set aside.

3. Remove the pork chops from the marinade and shake off any excess. Discard the marinade. Season both sides of the chops with the salt and pepper.

4. Supply your smoker with wood pellets and follow the manufacturer's specific start-up procedure. Preheat, with the lid closed, to 325°F.

5. Arrange the pork chops directly on the grill, close the lid, and smoke for 45 to 50 minutes, without flipping, until a meat thermometer inserted in the meat reads 160°F.

6. To serve, divide the chops among plates and top with the pickled pepper relish.

Smoking Tip Keep thinner chops from curling up by strategically making a few small cuts in the rim of fat surrounding the meat.

SOUTHERN SUGAR-GLAZED HAM

Serves 12 to 15

PREP TIME: 30 MINUTES
SMOKE TIME: 5 HOURS

 SMOKE
TEMPERATURE:
275°F

 WOOD PELLETS:
APPLE OR CHERRY

1 (12- to 15-pound) whole
bone-in ham, fully cooked

¼ cup yellow mustard

1 cup pineapple juice

½ cup packed light
brown sugar

1 teaspoon ground cinnamon

½ teaspoon ground cloves

Cooking a big, fat ham on your wood pellet grill is an easy way
to create that Norman Rockwell vibe for your next holiday feast.
It's easy because whole bone-in hams come fully cured and
cooked—just add smoke. Pound for pound, it makes for one
of the simplest, most elegant, and most affordable celebratory
meals. If you find an *uncured* ham, you can smoke it, too, but
it will, in fact, be a different dish. A smoked, uncured ham
(sometimes called a "green" ham) is best prepared like the
pork shoulder in Party Pulled Pork Shoulder (page 72).

1. Supply your smoker with wood pellets and follow the manufacturer's specific start-up procedure. Preheat, with the lid closed, to 275°F.

2. Trim off the excess fat and skin from the ham, leaving a ¼-inch layer of fat. Put the ham in an aluminum foil–lined roasting pan.

3. On your kitchen stovetop, in a medium saucepan over low heat, combine the mustard, pineapple juice, brown sugar, cinnamon, and cloves and simmer for 15 minutes, or until thick and reduced by about half.

4. Baste the ham with half of the pineapple–brown sugar syrup, reserving the rest for basting later in the cook.

5. Place the roasting pan on the grill, close the lid, and smoke for 4 hours.

6. Baste the ham with the remaining pineapple–brown sugar syrup and continue smoking with the lid closed for another hour, or until a meat thermometer inserted in the thickest part of the ham reads 140°F.

7. Remove the ham from the grill, tent with foil, and let rest for 20 minutes before carving.

Ingredient Tip A boneless ham will work with this method, too; however, cuts cooked bone-in tend to have more flavor.

Chapter 5

BEEF

Deep in the heart of Texas, the barbecue focus is pure beef. Of course, everything's bigger in Texas, so the stars of the show are hunks of beef brisket, massive shoulder clod, and Flintstones-esque beef ribs. Post oak wood is the popular choice for smokers like Aaron Franklin of Franklin Barbecue in Austin and Tim McLaughlin of Lockhart Smokehouse near Dallas. The beef and smoke flavors alone are so delicious, there's no real need for additional sauce or seasonings—just salt and pepper. In fact, some legendary Texas joints, like Kreuz Market in Lockhart, prohibit sauce! The same thinking applies at great steakhouses, where top-quality beef needs only salt, pepper, and smoke.

If you can't get to the Lone Star State, don't worry. Beef roams well beyond Texas. In California, the Santa Maria–style tri-tip is the defining protein on the grill. Check out my recipe for Oak-Smoke Tri-Tip (page 98) to see how it's done. ♦

◀ PERFECT FILETS, page 92, with TWICE-SMOKED POTATOES, page 150

CUTS AND QUALITY

Neighborhood butcher shops are hard to come by these days. The butcher at your supermarket can help, but you may have to seek out one of today's mail-order options to find what you need. Cuts that are best to smoke low and slow include brisket, shoulder clod, prime rib, beef ribs, and tri-tip.

Even the brisket has different "cuts" to it. The point and the flat are the brisket's two distinct muscle sections. The "flat" is a grainy slab of muscle fibers that is typically served sliced pencil-thin against the grain. The "point" is an attached group of muscle fibers that has no uniform grain and is considerably fattier than the flat. Serious barbecue joints will allow you to choose point or flat, and some even dice the point to serve as "burnt ends."

These days when I buy beef, I look for attributes like organic, hormone-free, and grass-fed, and for breeds like Wagyu. The cost of quality beef for barbecue continues to rise, and compared to chicken and pork, it can be downright expensive. But nothing tastes better than beef after a low-and-slow cook on a smoker. If it's good beef, all you really need to add is salt and pepper, but experimenting with different spices is rewarding as well.

Of course, most people shop at big grocery stores where it's difficult to find high-quality beef. Fortunately, today's trend of to-your-door delivery opens up a world of options, but you still need to watch out for shady steak salesmen who have moved from selling out of the back of an unmarked truck to Internet sales. The best beef providers include Snake River Farms (my favorite for brisket),

ButcherBox (grass-fed), and Allen Brothers (high-end steaks), and they change every so often. There are new players popping up every day, so I'll be sure to continue updating my recommendations at BarbecueTricks.com/resources.

GOOD GRADES

You have likely heard the saying "fat is flavor," and that is especially true when it comes to beef for the barbecue. There's actually a grading system that will give you a quick rating of a cut's features, including juiciness, tenderness, and flavor. To be honest, it's all simply about fat content, without regard to any of the attributes (like hormone-free) I mentioned earlier. You'll probably only ever see the grades "Choice" and "Select" in Wallyworld or supermarket chains, but here's the full list to broaden your horizons:

★ PRIME: This is the high-quality beef served in great steakhouses. You probably would want to avoid it if you are following a low-fat diet.

★ CHOICE: This is what you'll find most often in supermarkets. Because fat content is relative and you can usually see fat marbling through the packaging, Choice beef really comes off as more of a marketing term. It simply means meat that has less fat than what is labeled as Prime.

★ SELECT: It doesn't sound like it, but Select could be a positive if you seek a lean and low-fat source of protein.

- ★ STANDARD: You may find Standard in stores, but it will more likely just be "ungraded." Beware of misleading packaging that says Choice or Prime without USDA attribution.

- ★ OTHER: Cutter, Utility, and Canner labels denote lower quality. Stay away, because these cuts are nothing you want for barbecue.

TECHNIQUES

The three main techniques pit masters employ with beef have one thing in common: simplicity.

1. **Begin with good beef.** It could be a premium breed or simply a better cut. Special breeds like Wagyu have a higher percentage of delicious marbled fat. Like Ben Franklin said of beer, this is also proof that God loves us and wants us to be happy.

2. **Keep it simple.** Many of the best steakhouse chefs and brisket smoking masters season beef with nothing but salt and pepper. Don't overdo it.

3. **Wrap it up.** Wrapping large cuts like clod and brisket halfway through the cooking process can hold in moisture and soften the final product. Use heavy-duty aluminum foil (a.k.a. the Texas Crutch) or traditional pink butcher paper.

RULES TO GRILL BY

Individual cuts have special rules all their own. Overall, here are a few of the biggest to remember:

- ★ **Shop for quality.** The USDA grades of Prime, Choice, and Select mainly denote juicy fat content. Prime is not typically found in supermarkets. If you want the best, visit a real butcher shop.

- ★ **Don't fear the fat.** Fat is flavor. Just trim excessive fat caps that are thicker than a finger.

- ★ **Trust your grill.** Avoid opening your smoker to check progress. Every time you open the door or lift the lid, this drops the cook chamber's temperature and can extend total cook time dramatically—often by 15 to 20 minutes.

- ★ **Keep an eye on your temperature.** Brisket's internal temperature needs to hit 195°F to 205°F. Use an instant-read digital meat thermometer.

- ★ **If you're going to slice it, let it rest.** To retain those coveted juices, let the meat rest out of the cooker for at least 10 minutes before serving. It will also come up about 5 degrees during the rest period.

- ★ **Don't fret about the charred look of your roast.** If your wood pellet smoker is working right, it's not burned—that's bark, and it's amazing.

BACON-SWISS CHEESESTEAK MEATLOAF

Serves 8 to 10

PREP TIME: 15 MINUTES
SMOKE TIME: 2 HOURS

 SMOKE
TEMPERATURE:
225°F

 WOOD PELLETS:
HICKORY AND
MESQUITE

1 tablespoon canola oil

2 garlic cloves, finely chopped

1 medium onion,
finely chopped

1 poblano chile, stemmed,
seeded, and finely chopped

2 pounds extra-lean
ground beef

2 tablespoons Montreal steak
seasoning

1 tablespoon A.1. Steak Sauce

½ pound bacon, cooked and
crumbled

2 cups shredded Swiss cheese

1 egg, beaten

2 cups breadcrumbs

½ cup Tiger Sauce

Meatloaf is a favorite comfort food for the baby boomer generation. It gained popularity during the Great Depression as a way to stretch dinner budgets by utilizing leftovers and affordable ground beef. Meatloaf made on a smoker becomes even more comforting when it takes on the flavor of your favorite wood smoke.

1. On your stovetop, heat the canola oil in a medium sauté pan over medium-high heat. Add the garlic, onion, and poblano, and sauté for 3 to 5 minutes, or until the onion is just barely translucent.

2. Supply your smoker with wood pellets and follow the manufacturer's specific start-up procedure. Preheat, with the lid closed, to 225°F.

3. In a large bowl, combine the sautéed vegetables, ground beef, steak seasoning, steak sauce, bacon, Swiss cheese, egg, and breadcrumbs. Mix with your hands until well incorporated, then shape into a loaf.

4. Put the meatloaf in a cast iron skillet and place it on the grill. Close the lid and smoke for 2 hours, or until a meat thermometer inserted in the loaf reads 165°F.

5. Top with the meatloaf with the Tiger Sauce, remove from the grill, and let rest for about 10 minutes before serving.

Ingredient Tip Montreal steak seasoning is a coarse and distinct seasoning made of dehydrated garlic, paprika, granulated onion, coriander, and plenty of chunky sea salt and pepper. It is considered the perfect complement to steak. The varieties in the supermarket spice section are all good, but you can easily grind your own blend. Be sure to use whole peppercorns and sea salt to control your desired coarseness.

LONDON BROIL

Serves 3 to 4

MARINATING TIME: 4 HOURS
PREP TIME: 20 MINUTES
SMOKE TIME: 12 TO 16 MINUTES

 SMOKE
TEMPERATURE:
350°F

 WOOD PELLETS:
APPLE MASH BLEND
OR BBQ BLEND

1 (1½- to 2-pound) London broil
or top round steak

¼ cup soy sauce

2 tablespoons white wine

2 tablespoons extra-virgin
olive oil

¼ cup chopped scallions

2 tablespoons packed
brown sugar

2 garlic cloves, minced

2 teaspoons red pepper flakes

1 teaspoon freshly ground
black pepper

You'll often see meats labeled "London broil" at the market, but it's actually more of a *style* of steak than a type, marinated and grilled rare in the center, and sliced into strips against the grain. The actual cut is typically top round steak or flank steak. Tenderizing it with a meat mallet and marinating it for several hours helps the cheap cut of meat achieve higher status among steaks.

1. Using a meat mallet, pound the steak lightly all over on both sides to break down its fibers and tenderize. You are not trying to pound down the thickness.

2. In a medium bowl, make the marinade by combining the soy sauce, white wine, olive oil, scallions, brown sugar, garlic, red pepper flakes, and black pepper.

3. Put the steak in a shallow plastic container with a lid and pour the marinade over the meat. Cover and refrigerate for 4 hours.

4. Remove the steak from the marinade, shaking off any excess, and discard the marinade.

5. Supply your smoker with wood pellets and follow the manufacturer's specific start-up procedure. Preheat, with the lid closed, to 350°F.

6. Place the steak directly on the grill, close the lid, and smoke for 6 minutes. Flip, then smoke with the lid closed for 6 to 10 minutes more, or until a meat thermometer inserted in the meat reads 130°F for medium-rare.

7. Let the steak rest for about 10 minutes before slicing and serving. The meat's temperature will rise by about 5 degrees while it rests.

Smoking Tip To attain a hearty char, enlist the technique known as a "reverse sear." Cook as directed in step 6 until you are 5°F *under* the desired final internal target temperature. Then boost the grill to a high setting—such as 400°F to 450°F—to finish with a quick sear on both sides (about 1 minute per side).

BILL'S BEST FRENCH ONION BURGERS

Serves 4

PREP TIME: 35 MINUTES

SMOKE TIME: 20 TO 25 MINUTES

 SMOKE
TEMPERATURE:
425°F

 WOOD PELLETS:
OAK, MESQUITE,
OR HICKORY

1 pound lean ground beef

1 tablespoon minced garlic

1 teaspoon Better Than
Bouillon Beef Base

1 teaspoon dried chives

1 teaspoon freshly ground
black pepper

8 slices Gruyère
cheese, divided

½ cup soy sauce

1 tablespoon extra-virgin
olive oil

1 teaspoon liquid smoke

3 medium onions, cut into
thick slices (do not separate
the rings)

1 loaf French bread, cut into
8 slices

4 slices provolone cheese

French onion soup has a lot of the savory flavors I want in a burger. You could top a shoe with that hot, stringy cheese, and I'd want to pick off every last bit. I know it looks like there is a lot involved in this recipe for a simple burger, but I promise you won't be disappointed.

1. In a large bowl, mix together the ground beef, minced garlic, beef base, chives, and pepper until well blended.

2. Divide the meat mixture and shape into 8 thin burger patties.

3. Top each of 4 patties with one slice of Gruyère, then top with the remaining 4 patties to create 4 stuffed burgers.

4. Supply your smoker with wood pellets and follow the manufacturer's specific start-up procedure. Preheat, with the lid closed, to 425°F.

5. Arrange the burgers directly on one side of the grill, close the lid, and smoke for 10 minutes. Flip and smoke with the lid closed for 10 to 15 minutes more, or until a meat thermometer inserted in the burgers reads 160°F. Add another Gruyère slice to the burgers during the last 5 minutes of smoking to melt.

6. Meanwhile, in a small bowl, combine the soy sauce, olive oil, and liquid smoke.

7. Arrange the onion slices on the grill and baste on both sides with the soy sauce mixture. Smoke with the lid closed for 20 minutes, flipping halfway through.

8. Lightly toast the French bread slices on the grill. Layer each of 4 slices with a burger patty, a slice of provolone cheese, and some of the smoked onions. Top each with another slice of toasted French bread. Serve immediately.

Ingredient Tip Don't buy more than 80 percent lean ground beef to make hamburgers. An 80/20 lean-to-fat ratio makes for the tastiest burgers.

TEXAS SHOULDER CLOD

Serves 16 to 20

PREP TIME: 10 MINUTES

SMOKE TIME: 12 TO 16 HOURS

 SMOKE TEMPERATURE: 250°F

 WOOD PELLETS: OAK

½ cup sea salt

½ cup freshly ground black pepper

1 tablespoon red pepper flakes

1 tablespoon minced garlic

1 tablespoon cayenne pepper

1 tablespoon smoked paprika

1 (13- to 15-pound) beef shoulder clod

Beef shoulder clod is an affordable cut of beef made famous in select Texas smokehouses. The connective tissue requires a long, slow cook in order to break down to succulence. This massive hunk of beef feeds a crowd, but you can size down as needed. If you're cooking for 16 hours with a set-it-and-forget-it wood pellet grill smoker, you'll want to plan ahead. Have a beer and prepare a side dish (like the Twice-Smoked Potatoes on page 150). That should occupy half of your time, but you'll still have a few hours for a good book, gaming, or (if you're not careful) household chores.

1. In a small bowl, combine the salt, pepper, red pepper flakes, minced garlic, cayenne pepper, and smoked paprika to create a rub. Generously apply it to the beef shoulder.

2. Supply your smoker with wood pellets and follow the manufacturer's specific start-up procedure. Preheat, with the lid closed, to 250°F.

3. Put the meat on the grill grate, close the lid, and smoke for 12 to 16 hours, or until a meat thermometer inserted deeply into the beef reads 195°F. You may need to cover the clod with aluminum foil toward the end of smoking to prevent overbrowning.

4. Let the meat rest for about 15 minutes before slicing against the grain and serving.

Ingredient Tip Whole clod is hard to find. With more than five muscle groups coming together, at 15 pounds, it is often sold in smaller parts. It is also known as chuck arm pot roast, boneless shoulder cutlet, or arm chuck.

CORNED BEEF AND CABBAGE

Serves 6 to 8

SOAKING TIME: OVERNIGHT
PREP TIME: 30 MINUTES
SMOKE TIME: 4 TO 5 HOURS

 SMOKE
TEMPERATURE:
275°F

 WOOD PELLETS:
OAK OR HICKORY

FOR THE CORNED BEEF

1 gallon water

1 (3- to 4-pound) point cut
corned beef brisket with
pickling spice packet

1 tablespoon freshly ground
black pepper

1 tablespoon garlic powder

½ cup molasses

1 teaspoon ground mustard

FOR THE CABBAGE

1 head green cabbage

4 tablespoons (½ stick) butter

2 tablespoons rendered
bacon fat

1 chicken bouillon
cube, crushed

Corned beef is beef brisket that has been "corned," which is another word for wet cured, or brined. You'll find whole briskets available for purchase already soaked in the corning solution. This brine traditionally has salt, curing salt, sugar, garlic, pickling spices, and water. These days, many supermarkets sell smaller brisket cuts packaged along with the curing spices to make this process much easier. It is true that a smoked corned beef is usually considered pastrami, but the presentation here is more like the traditional Irish-American dish, with a lick of smoke. Head to the Homemade Pastrami recipe (page 93) for the deli sandwich favorite.

TO MAKE THE CORNED BEEF

1. In a large container with a lid, combine the water and the corned beef pickling spice packet and submerge the corned beef in it. Cover and refrigerate overnight, changing the water as often as you remember to do so—ideally, every 3 hours while you're awake—to soak out some of the curing salt originally added.

2. Supply your smoker with wood pellets and follow the manufacturer's specific start-up procedure. Preheat, with the lid closed, to 275°F.

3. Remove the meat from the brining liquid, pat it dry, and generously rub with the black pepper and garlic powder.

4. Put the seasoned corned beef directly on the grill, fat-side up, close the lid, and grill for 2 hours. Remove from the grill when done.

5. In a small bowl, combine the molasses and ground mustard and pour half of this mixture into the bottom of a disposable aluminum pan.

6. Transfer the meat to the pan, fat-side up, and pour the remaining molasses mixture on top, spreading it evenly over the meat. Cover tightly with aluminum foil.

7. Transfer the pan to the grill, close the lid, and continue smoking the corned beef for 2 to 3 hours, or until a meat thermometer inserted in the thickest part reads 185°F.

1. While the brisket is smoking, core the cabbage and fill the resulting cavity with the butter, rendered bacon fat, and crushed chicken bouillon cube.

2. Wrap the cabbage in foil about two-thirds of the way up the sides to protect the outer leaves, but do not completely cover, and place on the grill alongside the corned beef about an hour before the meat is expected to be finished.

3. Remove both the corned beef and the cabbage from the grill. Let the meat rest for 15 minutes, then slice against the grain.

4. Carefully unwrap the cabbage and pour the compound butter from the cavity into a large casserole dish.

5. Chop the cabbage and add to the casserole dish, then top with the sliced corned beef to serve.

Technique Tip The main difference between corned beef and pastrami is that the former is boiled and the latter is smoked. We're breaking the rule here and smoking corned beef anyway with different seasonings.

CHEESEBURGER HAND PIES

Makes 6

PREP TIME: 35 MINUTES

SMOKE TIME: 10 MINUTES

 SMOKE
TEMPERATURE:
325°F

 WOOD PELLETS:
HICKORY

½ pound lean ground beef

1 tablespoon minced onion

1 tablespoon steak seasoning

1 cup shredded Monterey Jack
and Colby cheese blend

8 slices white American
cheese, divided

2 (14-ounce) refrigerated
prepared pizza dough
sheets, divided

2 eggs, beaten with
2 tablespoons water (egg
wash), divided

24 hamburger dill pickle chips

2 tablespoons sesame seeds

6 slices tomato, for garnish

Ketchup and mustard,
for serving

Sometimes an idea sounds too good not to try. Consider this a poor man's beef Wellington . . . or maybe more of an upscale Hot Pocket. I tried using filo dough and piecrust dough before settling on rectangular sheets of pizza dough as the way to go. I got the best results using Pillsbury refrigerated pizza dough. Be sure to start with chilled dough, as it will make for much easier handling.

1. Supply your smoker with wood pellets and follow the manufacturer's specific start-up procedure. Preheat, with the lid closed, to 325°F.

2. On your stovetop, in a medium sauté pan over medium-high heat, brown the ground beef for 4 to 5 minutes, or until cooked through. Add the minced onion and steak seasoning.

3. Toss in the shredded cheese blend and 2 slices of American cheese, and stir until melted and fully incorporated.

4. Remove the cheeseburger mixture from the heat and set aside.

5. Make sure the dough is well chilled for easier handling. Working quickly, roll out one prepared pizza crust on parchment paper and brush with half of the egg wash.

6. Arrange the remaining 6 slices of American cheese on the dough to outline 6 hand pies.

7. Top each cheese slice with ¼ cup of the cheeseburger mixture, spreading slightly inside the imaginary lines of the hand pies.

8. Place 4 pickle slices on top of the filling for each pie.

9. Top the whole thing with the other prepared pizza crust and cut between the cheese slices to create 6 hand pies.

10. Using kitchen scissors, cut the parchment to further separate the pies, but leave them on the paper.

11. Using a fork dipped in egg wash, seal the edges of the pies on all sides. Baste the tops of the pies with the remaining egg wash and sprinkle with the sesame seeds.

12. Remove the pies from the parchment paper and gently place on the grill grate. Close the lid and smoke for 5 minutes, then carefully flip and smoke with the lid closed for 5 more minutes, or until browned.

13. Top with the sliced tomato and serve with ketchup and mustard.

Pair It **Serve this American meat pie in paradise with Sweet Potato Chips (page 152).**

PERFECT FILETS

Serves 2

PREP TIME: 10 MINUTES

SMOKE TIME: 12 TO 14 MINUTES

 SMOKE
TEMPERATURE:
450°F

 WOOD PELLETS:
OAK OR PECAN

2 (1¼-inch-thick) filet mignons

2 teaspoons sea salt

2 teaspoons freshly ground
black pepper

2 teaspoons minced garlic

2 teaspoons onion powder

Lately I've been spending a lot of money so my family can eat grass-fed organic steaks. Heck, when I was a kid, *everything* was organic! One great feature of wood pellet grills is that they get hot enough to give expensive steaks the attention they deserve. Dial it up to high to treat your filet to the perfect amount of smoke and sear. Have I mentioned that I love pellet power?

1. Supply your smoker with wood pellets and follow the manufacturer's specific start-up procedure. Preheat, with the lid closed, to 450°F.

2. In a small bowl, combine the salt, pepper, minced garlic, and onion powder to form a rub, and generously apply it to both sides of the steaks.

3. Lay the steaks on grill grate, close the lid, and smoke for 7 minutes. Flip and continue smoking with the lid closed for 5 to 7 minutes, or until the internal temperature reaches 125°F to 130°F for medium-rare. Remove the steaks from the grill. (Don't worry if the temperature is 5°F under the desired temperature when you remove the steak from the grill. The temperature will increase slightly during the rest period.)

4. Let the meat rest for 5 minutes before serving.

Pair It Serve these steaks with Twice-Smoked Potatoes (page 150).

HOMEMADE PASTRAMI

Serves 12

SOAKING TIME: OVERNIGHT

REFRIGERATION TIME: 1 HOUR
BEFORE SLICING TO SERVE

PREP TIME: 10 MINUTES

SMOKE TIME: 4 TO 5 HOURS

 SMOKE
TEMPERATURE:
275°F

 WOOD PELLETS:
OAK OR HICKORY

1 gallon water, plus ½ cup

½ cup packed light
brown sugar

1 (3- to 4-pound) point cut
corned beef brisket with brine
mix packet

2 tablespoons freshly ground
black pepper

¼ cup ground coriander

The famous "I'll have what she's having" scene from *When Harry Met Sally* was filmed at what is the world pastrami headquarters: the 125-year-old Katz's Delicatessen in New York City's Lower East Side. A coriander-heavy crust is a hallmark of this brisket in disguise.

1. In a large container with a lid, combine 1 gallon of water, the brown sugar, and the corned beef spice packet, then submerge the corned beef in it. Cover and refrigerate overnight, changing the water as often as you remember to do so—ideally, every 3 hours while you're awake—to soak out some of the curing salt originally added.

2. Supply your smoker with wood pellets and follow the manufacturer's specific start-up procedure. Preheat, with the lid closed, to 275°F.

3. In a small bowl, combine the black pepper and ground coriander to form a rub.

4. Drain the meat, pat it dry, and generously coat on all sides with the rub.

5. Place the corned beef directly on the grill, fat-side up, close the lid, and smoke for 3 hours to 3 hours 30 minutes, or until a meat thermometer inserted in the thickest part reads 175°F to 185°F.

6. Pour the remaining ½ cup of water into the bottom of a disposable roasting pan. Add the corned beef, cover tightly with aluminum foil, and smoke on the grill with the lid closed for an additional 30 minutes to 1 hour.

7. Remove the meat from the grill and let cool for about 10 minutes. Transfer to a plate and refrigerate for at least 1 hour before thinly slicing and serving.

Ingredient Tip Like with any brisket, you'll want to keep track of how the meat fibers run and be sure to slice as thinly as possible perpendicular to, or "against," the grain.

ROAST BEAST

Serves 6 to 8

PREP TIME: 10 MINUTES

SMOKE TIME: 3 TO 4 HOURS (ABOUT 1 HOUR PER POUND)

 SMOKE TEMPERATURE: 425°F, 225°F

 WOOD PELLETS: OAK, MESQUITE, OR TENNESSEE WHISKEY BARREL BLEND

1 (3- to 4-pound) rump roast

Extra-virgin olive oil, for rubbing

2 tablespoons steak seasoning

1 tablespoon minced garlic

Most of the smoking of this roast is done low and slow at 225°F, but a favorite trick for wood pellet grill owners is to start the process with a quick surface sear. With just a few minutes of hot-and-fast roasting, you can lock in juices and give the crust a head start. Any leftovers will slice up nicely for sandwiches.

1. Supply your smoker with wood pellets and follow the manufacturer's specific start-up procedure. Preheat, with the lid closed, to 425°F.

2. Rub the roast with olive oil and generously apply steak seasoning and minced garlic.

3. Put the meat directly on the grill and sear all surfaces of the roast for 2 to 5 minutes per side. Remove from the grill.

4. Reduce the temperature to 225°F.

5. Place the roast back on the grill, close the lid, and smoke for 3 to 4 hours, or until a meat thermometer inserted in the thickest part of the roast reads 120°F to 155°F, based on your desired doneness. (See the chart on page 24.)

6. Remove the roast from the grill, tent with aluminum foil, and let rest for about 10 minutes before slicing against the grain to serve.

Smoking Tip Be alert at the end of the cook. You want to avoid overcooking. Keep in mind that the roast's temperature will continue to rise several degrees as it rests.

CRISPY BURNT ENDS

Serves 6

PREP TIME: 15 MINUTES

SMOKE TIME: 8 HOURS

 SMOKE
TEMPERATURE:
275°F

 WOOD PELLETS:
OAK OR HICKORY

1 (3-pound) chuck roast

3 tablespoons Our House Dry
Rub (page 190)

¾ cup Bill's Best BBQ Sauce
(page 183), divided

Burnt ends are a treat said to have originated long ago in a Kansas City restaurant. The throwaway scraps became so popular, they were soon in high demand. Usually cubed from the fatty point end of a brisket, burnt ends have now become almost mandatory for competition brisket submissions. This recipe mimics the beefy bark of brisket, but calls for the more affordable yet fatty chuck roast. The trick is to render down the fat to achieve a melt-in-your-mouth, sweet-and-savory bite.

1. Supply your smoker with wood pellets and follow the manufacturer's specific start-up procedure. Preheat, with the lid closed, to 275°F.

2. Liberally season the chuck roast with the dry rub.

3. Place the meat directly on the grill, close the lid, and smoke for about 5 hours, or until you see a dark bark on the surface of the meat and a meat thermometer inserted in the thickest part reads 165°F.

4. Wrap the meat tightly in aluminum foil and continue smoking with the lid closed for about another hour, or until the internal temperature registers 195°F on the meat thermometer.

5. Remove from the heat and let rest for 15 to 20 minutes before cutting into 2-inch cubes.

6. Transfer the cubes to a disposable baking pan and toss with ½ cup of barbecue sauce.

7. Place the pan on the grill, close the lid, and smoke for another 1 hour 30 minutes to 2 hours, or until hot and bubbly, adding the remaining ¼ cup of barbecue sauce in the last 30 minutes of cooking.

8. Serve immediately.

Smoking Tip Pit masters will argue about how sweet burnt ends should be. Most prefer them with a sweet sauce like the one we use in this recipe. If you use one that's less sweet, you can always toss in some brown sugar in step 6.

SMOKED PRIME RIB

Serves 6 to 8

PREP TIME: 15 MINUTES

SMOKE TIME: 20 MINUTES PER POUND

 SMOKE TEMPERATURE: 450°F, 300°F

 WOOD PELLETS: OAK OR PECAN

1 (3- to 4-pound) prime rib

Butcher's string

1 tablespoon coarse salt

1 tablespoon freshly ground black pepper

1 tablespoon garlic powder

Chimichurri Sauce (page 184), for serving

The prime rib is the king of all beef roasts, called prime because it is *premium*, not necessarily because of its USDA grade. Cooking bone-in is the way to go, as that almost always results in more flavor.

1. Let the roast sit at room temperature for about 1 hour, then tie with butcher's string in several places to hold it together during the smoking process.

2. Supply your smoker with wood pellets and follow the manufacturer's specific start-up procedure. Preheat, with the lid closed, to 450°F.

3. In a small bowl, combine the salt, pepper, and garlic powder, and rub this mixture all over the prime rib.

4. Place the meat bone-side down in a roasting pan with a rack and put the pan on the grill.

5. Close the lid and smoke the prime rib for 30 minutes, then reduce the heat to 300°F.

6. Continue to roast the meat with the lid closed for 25 to 50 minutes, depending on the size and desired internal temperature. Total cook time will be about 20 minutes per pound, but do not remove from the heat before a meat thermometer inserted deep into the middle of the meat reads between 120°F (rare) and 155°F (well-done).

7. Let the prime rib rest for 10 to 20 minutes before removing the string and removing the bones.

8. Slice the steak, transfer to plates, and serve drizzled with chimichurri sauce.

Technique Tip Use caution if you like your beef more on the rare side, as it will continue to cook and the internal temperature will rise for a few minutes even after you remove it from the grill.

T-BONE TONIGHT WITH BLUE CHEESE BUTTER

Serves 4

PREP TIME: 10 MINUTES

SMOKE TIME: 45 TO 50 MINUTES

 SMOKE
TEMPERATURE:
165°F, 450°F

 WOOD PELLETS:
HICKORY

4 tablespoons (½ stick) unsalted butter, at room temperature

½ cup blue cheese crumbles

4 (14-ounce, 1-inch-thick) T-bone steaks

2 tablespoons kosher salt

1 tablespoon freshly ground black pepper

2 tablespoons minced garlic

The macho T-bone is my favorite steaks. Yes, I said "steaks," because it's really two steak cuts in one. On one side, you get the succulent and fatty New York strip; on the other, you get a lean and tender filet mignon. Yep, we're throwing portion control to the wind tonight! Cooking anything with the bone in always enhances the flavor in inexplicable ways, and the roasting adds something magical to the morsels closest to the bone. Plus, it just looks so awesomely cool.

1. In a medium bowl, stir together the butter and blue cheese crumbles and set aside, but do not refrigerate unless making in advance.

2. Supply your smoker with wood pellets and follow the manufacturer's specific start-up procedure. Preheat, with the lid closed, to 165°F.

3. Season the steaks with the salt, pepper, and garlic.

4. Arrange the steaks directly on the grill, close the lid, and smoke for 30 minutes.

5. Increase the heat to 450°F and smoke for an additional 15 minutes for medium-rare, or longer for desired doneness, turning once, until a meat thermometer inserted in the meat reads 120°F to 155°F.

6. Remove the steaks from the grill and let rest for 3 to 5 minutes before serving topped with the blue cheese butter.

Pair It   Cowboy up with a rustic side dish that's bold enough to share the plate with a T-bone: Carolina Baked Beans (page 158).

OAK-SMOKE TRI-TIP

Serves 4 to 6

PREP TIME: 15 MINUTES

SMOKE TIME: 45 MINUTES TO
1 HOUR

 SMOKE
TEMPERATURE:
425°F

 WOOD PELLETS:
OAK

2 teaspoons sea salt

2 teaspoons freshly ground
black pepper

2 teaspoons onion powder

2 teaspoons garlic powder

2 teaspoons dried oregano

1 teaspoon cayenne pepper

1 teaspoon ground sage

1 teaspoon finely chopped
fresh rosemary

1 (1½ – to 2-pound) tri-tip
bottom sirloin

In California, the Santa Maria–style tri-tip is legendary. The pit masters of the Santa Maria Valley in central California focus on the triangular-shaped roast from the lower area of the sirloin. Unlike brisket, this beef is typically wood-fired over a live fire of red oak, using a unique and very cool grill grate that can be raised and lowered to adjust the heat. Also unlike brisket, this is best served medium-rare with an herb-heavy dry rub. Tri-tip may also be found in supermarkets under the alias "triangle steak."

1. Supply your smoker with wood pellets and follow the manufacturer's specific start-up procedure. Preheat, with the lid closed, to 425°F.

2. In a small bowl, combine the salt, pepper, onion powder, garlic powder, oregano, cayenne pepper, sage, and rosemary to create a rub.

3. Season the meat all over with the rub and lay it directly on the grill.

4. Close the lid and smoke for 45 minutes to 1 hour, or until a meat thermometer inserted in the thickest part of the meat reads 120°F for rare, 130°F for medium-rare, or 140°F for medium, keeping in mind that the meat will come up in temperature by about another 5°F during the rest period.

5. Remove the tri-tip from the heat, tent with aluminum foil, and let rest for 15 minutes before slicing against the grain.

Pair It In California, the traditional side dish for tri-tip is savory pinquito beans, along with salsa. The pinquito is in the same family as the pinto bean but is harder to find. We tracked them down at RanchoGordo.com, an online specialty food shop that offers an unmatched variety of heirloom beans.

WEEKNIGHT STUFFED PEPPERS

Serves 4

PREP TIME: 30 MINUTES

SMOKE TIME: 1 HOUR 15 MINUTES

 SMOKE TEMPERATURE: 350°F

 WOOD PELLETS: MESQUITE

4 large bell peppers, tops removed, cored, and seeded

½ pound ground beef

½ pound ground sausage

1 large onion, diced

1 poblano chile, stemmed, seeded, and finely chopped

1 (14-ounce) can tomato paste

1½ cups grated Cheddar cheese, divided

1 teaspoon seasoned salt

1 teaspoon freshly ground black pepper

1 tablespoon minced garlic

Whether it's a tortilla bowl or a waffle cone, who doesn't love a bowl you can eat? You'll definitely still need a plate for this dish, though. Experiment with yellow and red bell peppers for color variety. You can keep them more stable on the grill grate by wrapping the base of each pepper with a ring fashioned out of aluminum foil. This stuffed pepper makes the perfect individual portion.

1. Place the peppers in a disposable aluminum pan, wrapping them at the base with aluminum foil rings, if necessary, to keep them stable.

2. Supply your smoker with wood pellets and follow the manufacturer's specific start-up procedure. Preheat, with the lid closed, to 350°F.

3. On your stovetop, in a large skillet over medium-high heat, brown the ground beef and ground sausage together for 5 to 7 minutes; drain off the fat and crumble the meat.

4. Stir the onion, poblano chile, tomato paste, 1 cup of Cheddar cheese, salt, pepper, and garlic into the meat, mixing well.

5. Stuff the bell peppers in the aluminum pan with the meat mixture.

6. Place the pan on the grill, close the lid, and smoke for 1 hour.

7. Top the stuffed peppers with the remaining ½ cup of cheese and continue smoking with the lid closed for 15 minutes, then remove from the heat.

8. Serve hot.

Substitution Tip For a spicier version, try substituting chorizo for the ground beef.

ULTIMATE BRISKET

Serves 8 to 12

PREP TIME: 35 MINUTES

SMOKE TIME: 8 TO 10 HOURS

 SMOKE
TEMPERATURE:
225°F

 WOOD PELLETS:
OAK

1 cup kosher salt

1 cup coarsely ground
black pepper

1 (8- to 12-pound) brisket,
most fat trimmed off

1 cup yellow mustard

1 cup apple cider vinegar

1 cup apple juice

2 tablespoons salt

Pink butcher paper

Fatty beef brisket is considered the king of barbecue. But it wasn't always such a superstar. In Depression-era Texas, brisket, the tough and grainy chest muscle of the cow, was considered a cheap cut—but no longer. Today, it's the cornerstone meat of Texas barbecue, and is one of the most glamorous categories in competition barbecue. Why is it so popular? One bite explains it. In fact, when the real world starts getting me down, I remind myself, "You can't please everyone; you're not brisket."

1. Supply your smoker with wood pellets and follow the manufacturer's specific start-up procedure. Preheat, with the lid closed, to 225°F.

2. In a small bowl, combine the salt and pepper.

3. Slather the trimmed brisket with the mustard, then generously apply the salt and pepper mixture to the meat until it's well coated. (It's a lot, but with a brisket this size, you need it.)

4. Place the meat in the center of the grill, fat-side up. Close the lid and smoke for 4 to 5 hours, or until a meat thermometer inserted in the thickest part of the meat reads 165°F.

5. While the brisket is smoking, make the mop sauce. In a bowl, combine the apple cider vinegar, apple juice, and salt, and pour into a spray bottle.

6. When the brisket has finished the first 4 to 5 hours of cooking, spray it with the mop sauce and wrap tightly with pink butcher paper to seal in the juices. Close the lid and continue smoking for another 4 to 5 hours (or longer as needed), spraying with the mop sauce every hour. You're looking for an internal temperature of 195°F to 205°F, and the brisket should have a nice dark bark.

7. Remove the meat from the grill, unwrap it, and let rest for up to an hour before slicing.

8. Separate the point side by dividing at the fat line. Shred or reserve for burnt ends. (Cut into 2-inch cubes, toss in barbecue sauce, and heat in a foil pan until sticky and hot. See the process I used with chuck roast in Crispy Burnt Ends on page 95.)

9. Cut the flat-shaped half of the brisket against the grain into thin slices.

Ingredient Tip We've all heard the saying "fat is flavor," but you'll still want to trim some of the exorbitant fat from this mega cut before cooking. A good rule of thumb is to use your finger. That is, trim off fat to a remaining thickness equal to the width of your finger. The low-and-slow cooking should do the rest of the work to dissolve the fat that's left.

Chapter 6
FISH AND SEAFOOD

Salmon is by far the most popular fish to smoke. These days, we're even seeing it at the market alongside traditional beef jerky. Its oily flesh makes it the perfect canvas for absorbing smoke flavor. But there's an endless variety of seafood that can also take on smoke incredibly well. The rule of thumb is the fattier the fish, the more smoky flavor you'll taste. Salmon and trout have high fat content and are ideal for wood pellet smokers. That's because the smokers allow you to easily maintain the lower, sub-200°F temperatures that let the fish slowly absorb the subtle wood flavors—without fear of overcooking the delicate flesh. As with smoked meats, the process of smoking fish started as a way of not only cooking, but also of preserving the food. The bold flavors and superior health benefits continue to stand the test of time. ◑

◀ SUMMER PAELLA, page I22

103

CUTS

The lightness of seafood is a perfect match for wood pellet smokers. The light flesh picks up subtle flavors nicely, and because most seafood is quick to cook, the lower temperature settings of pellet grills can help prevent overcooking.

Living on the coast of South Carolina, I firmly believe that the best seafood for your smoker depends on where you live. Shopping local means you can get the freshest product possible. Shrimp is my local favorite, and there are plenty of ways to prepare it (just ask Bubba Gump for his list). Lobster is an uncommon but elegant treat on the smoker that is much easier to prepare than you may think. Smoked fish is another staple of the pellet smoker. Salmon to tuna, the oilier the fish, the better for absorbing smoke flavor. Oysters and hardwood smoke are also a great combination—you can host a real oyster roast instead of serving the more typical steamed oysters. Here, we roast them on the half shell topped with a seasoned butter.

One other consideration with fish and seafood is what's in season where you live. But don't let locale or seasonality deter you too much from what you crave. Good markets, modern seafood farming, and modern distribution make most seafood accessible year-round.

TECHNIQUE

Smoking fish with the skin on can help the flesh retain moisture, but you don't want to eat all kinds of fish skin. Many people love the taste of salmon skin when fried crisp. Pellet smoking will not crisp the skin to many people's liking, but you'll still want to leave it on one side of the fillet to allow for easier maneuverability on the grill.

 At the Fish Market

Shopping for fish can seem complicated. More than just type, you have to decide on whole or cleaned, farm-raised or local, fresh or frozen.

When shopping for fresh fish, look with your nose first. Fresh fish should smell clean and briny, not "off" or overly fishy. The eyes should appear shiny and full, not cloudy or sunken. Skin and scales should look shiny and metallic. With fillets, flesh should be firm and bright (not dull)—and *never* slimy.

RULES TO GRILL BY

Fish over wood fire is one of the greatest combinations in culinary history. But there are a few things to keep in mind for seafood success:

★ Use kosher salt in these recipes, not table salt. The latter may contain iodide and anti-caking agents that can give fish an off flavor.

★ Blotting and drying the surface of the pre-smoked fish fillet allows for the formation of a pellicle, a sticky, thin, lacquer-like film on the surface of the fish that helps smoke adhere to the meat.

★ Choose skin-off fillets or thin-skinned fish for the best absorption of smoke flavors.

★ While cleaning (and before seasoning), use your fingers to inspect fish fillets like salmon and trout for pin bones and remove them.

★ Fish is notorious for messy cleanup. Use aluminum foil (pierced with vent holes) or Frogmats to minimize hassle.

★ Enlist the help of a grill basket to protect the flesh of the fish, or place pieces skin-side down on the grate.

★ Light-flavored foods call for more delicate and aromatic wood flavors. Fruit and alder wood pellets are fish favorites

★ A fish spatula is slotted, thin, and flexible, making it the perfect tool for lifting and moving delicate pieces of fish.

★ Use tongs and a cloth or paper towel dipped in vegetable oil to brush oil on the grill grate to prevent sticking.

CHARLESTON CRAB CAKES WITH REMOULADE

Serves 4

PREP TIME: 30 MINUTES

SMOKE TIME: 45 MINUTES

 SMOKE
TEMPERATURE:
375°F

 WOOD PELLETS:
APPLE

If you've ever handpicked a blue crab, you know what a luxury food a crab cake is. It's an extra-nice treat when someone else has done the hard handpicking work. Remoulade may seem a bit fancy for beach food, but top as you like. A remoulade is a French condiment that is aioli- or mayonnaise-based, and I like to think of it as a distant cousin of tartar sauce.

FOR THE REMOULADE

1¼ cups mayonnaise

¼ cup yellow mustard

2 tablespoons sweet pickle relish, with its juices

1 tablespoon smoked paprika

2 teaspoons Cajun seasoning

2 teaspoons prepared horseradish

1 teaspoon hot sauce

1 garlic clove, finely minced

FOR THE CRAB CAKES

2 pounds fresh lump crabmeat, picked clean

20 butter crackers (such as Ritz brand), crushed

2 tablespoons Dijon mustard

1 cup mayonnaise

2 tablespoons freshly squeezed lemon juice

1 tablespoon salted butter, melted

1 tablespoon Worcestershire sauce

1 tablespoon Old Bay seasoning

2 teaspoons chopped fresh parsley

1 teaspoon ground mustard

2 eggs, beaten

¼ cup extra-virgin olive oil, divided

TO MAKE THE REMOULADE

1. In a small bowl, combine the mayonnaise, mustard, pickle relish, paprika, Cajun seasoning, horseradish, hot sauce, and garlic.

2. Refrigerate until ready to serve.

TO MAKE THE CRAB CAKES

1. Supply your smoker with wood pellets and follow the manufacturer's specific start-up procedure. Preheat, with the lid closed, to 375°F.

2. Spread the crabmeat on a foil-lined baking sheet and place over indirect heat on the grill, with the lid closed, for 30 minutes.

3. Remove from the heat and let cool for 15 minutes.

4. While the crab cools, combine the crushed crackers, Dijon mustard, mayonnaise, lemon juice, melted butter, Worcestershire sauce, Old Bay, parsley, ground mustard, and eggs until well incorporated.

5. Fold in the smoked crabmeat, then shape the mixture into 8 (1-inch-thick) crab cakes.

6. In a large skillet or cast-iron pan on the grill, heat 2 tablespoons of olive oil. Add half of the crab cakes, close the lid, and smoke for 4 to 5 minutes on each side, or until crispy and golden brown.

7. Remove the crab cakes from the pan and transfer to a wire rack to drain. Pat them to remove any excess oil.

8. Repeat steps 6 and 7 with the remaining oil and crab cakes.

9. Serve the crab cakes with the remoulade.

Ingredient Tip If you're shopping for crab and instead find "krab," steer clear. Imitation crab is widely available in all shapes and sizes, but it doesn't hold a candle to the real deal.

CITRUS-SMOKED TROUT

Serves 6 to 8

BRINING TIME: 1 HOUR

PREP TIME: 10 MINUTES

SMOKE TIME: 1 HOUR 30 MINUTES
TO 2 HOURS

 SMOKE
TEMPERATURE:
225°F

 WOOD PELLETS:
ALDER OR OAK

6 to 8 skin-on rainbow trout,
cleaned and scaled

1 gallon orange juice

½ cup packed light
brown sugar

¼ cup salt

1 tablespoon freshly ground
black pepper

Nonstick spray, oil, or butter,
for greasing

1 tablespoon chopped
fresh parsley

1 lemon, sliced

Have you heard that goldfish can be overfed and die because they don't know when to stop eating? Similarly, trout spend about 80 percent of their day foraging for food and eating. No wonder I can relate to them. Trout are generally plentiful and, as members of the salmon family, they grow fairly large. The biggest rainbow trout on record was caught in Canada in 2009, weighing in at 48 pounds!

1. Fillet the fish and pat dry with paper towels.

2. Pour the orange juice into a large container with a lid and stir in the brown sugar, salt, and pepper.

3. Place the trout in the brine, cover, and refrigerate for 1 hour.

4. Cover the grill grate with heavy-duty aluminum foil. Poke holes in the foil and spray with cooking spray (see Tip).

5. Supply your smoker with wood pellets and follow the manufacturer's specific start-up procedure. Preheat, with the lid closed, to 225°F.

6. Remove the trout from the brine and pat dry. Arrange the fish on the foil-covered grill grate, close the lid, and smoke for 1 hour 30 minutes to 2 hours, or until flaky.

7. Remove the fish from the heat. Serve garnished with the fresh parsley and lemon slices.

Smoking Tip Fish has a tendency to stick to the grill, so to aid in cleanup, cover the grate with heavy-duty aluminum foil. Poke holes in the foil so the smoke can get through, and spray with nonstick spray to further prevent sticking. You could also use a greased Frogmat. (Wish I had invented those. . . .) Here we are filleting and smoking a more typical trout. You can see a concise fillet method at FoodandWine.com/video/how-fillet-trout.

WEEKEND CAJUN SHRIMP

Serves 6 to 8

PREP TIME: 15 MINUTES

SMOKE TIME: 30 TO 45 MINUTES

 SMOKE
TEMPERATURE:
250°F

 WOOD PELLETS:
MESQUITE OR
HICKORY

2 cups (2 sticks) unsalted butter, melted

1⅛ cups Tabasco sauce

3 tablespoons salt

3 tablespoons Cajun seasoning

3 tablespoons cayenne pepper

1 tablespoon red pepper flakes

1 tablespoon dried rosemary

3 pounds tail-on jumbo shrimp, peeled and deveined

Juice of 1 lemon

¼ cup chopped fresh parsley, for garnish

1 loaf French bread, torn into pieces, for serving

My brother-in-law, Paul Stewart of Palmetto Bay Sunrise Café on Hilton Head Island, is the master of she-crab soup and also of shrimp. It's tough to grill soup, so I figured I would share his shrimp recipe instead. With all the Cajun-inspired heat in this dish, you'll want to have a cold beer handy. It's also important to use a strong wood smoke for this recipe. The shrimp cook fast, so you'll need a wood that imparts flavor quickly.

1. Supply your smoker with wood pellets and follow the manufacturer's specific start-up procedure. Preheat, with the lid closed, to 250°F.

2. In a small bowl, combine the butter, Tabasco, salt, Cajun seasoning, cayenne, red pepper flakes, and rosemary.

3. Place the shrimp in a disposable aluminum foil pan with high sides.

4. Pour the butter mixture over the shrimp and place the pan on the grill grate.

5. Smoke over direct heat, with the lid closed, for 30 to 45 minutes, or until the shrimp are pink and the butter is bubbling.

6. Squeeze the lemon juice over the shrimp and sprinkle the parsley on top.

7. Serve hot with torn bread to sop up the spicy butter.

Ingredient Tip Keep an eye on your shrimp. Undercooked shrimp will retain a straight shape. If they're overcooked, you'll see them curl up into the dreaded "O" shape. You want to aim for a nicely cooked "C" shape. C students rejoice!

DELICIOUS DEVILED CRAB APPETIZER

Makes 30 mini crab cakes

PREP TIME: 20 MINUTES

SMOKE TIME: 10 MINUTES

 SMOKE
TEMPERATURE:
425°F

 WOOD PELLETS:
PECAN

Nonstick cooking spray, oil, or
butter, for greasing

1 cup panko
breadcrumbs, divided

1 cup canned corn, drained

½ cup chopped
scallions, divided

½ red bell pepper,
finely chopped

16 ounces jumbo lump
crabmeat

¾ cup mayonnaise, divided

1 egg, beaten

1 teaspoon salt

1 teaspoon freshly ground
black pepper

2 teaspoons cayenne
pepper, divided

Juice of 1 lemon

The origin story of deviled crab is tied to smoke—cigar smoke, actually. The discovery of deviled crab has been traced back to a cigar workers' strike in Ybor City, Florida, in the 1920s. I remember having deviled crab as a kid, and it was served in a crab-shaped tin. We prepare it below using a mini muffin pan, but you could just as easily use a real hollowed-out crab shell, find manufactured crab shell tins online, or prepare as small cakes, with no shell, on a baking sheet.

1. Supply your smoker with wood pellets and follow the manufacturer's specific start-up procedure. Preheat, with the lid closed, to 425°F.

2. Spray three 12-cup mini muffin pans with cooking spray and divide ½ cup of the panko between 30 of the muffin cups, pressing into the bottoms and up the sides. (Work in batches, if necessary, depending on the number of pans you have.)

3. In a medium bowl, combine the corn, ¼ cup of scallions, the bell pepper, crabmeat, half of the mayonnaise, the egg, salt, pepper, and 1 teaspoon of cayenne pepper.

4. Gently fold in the remaining ½ cup of breadcrumbs and divide the mixture between the prepared mini muffin cups.

5. Place the pans on the grill grate, close the lid, and smoke for 10 minutes, or until golden brown.

6. In a small bowl, combine the lemon juice and the remaining mayonnaise, scallions, and cayenne pepper to make a sauce.

7. Brush the tops of the mini crab cakes with the sauce and serve hot.

Pair It Combine this deviled crab appetizer with a platter of Bacon-Wrapped Jalapeño Poppers (page 163) for a finger-food feast.

DIJON-SMOKED HALIBUT

Serves 4

MARINATING TIME: 4 HOURS
PREP TIME: 20 MINUTES
SMOKE TIME: 2 HOURS

 SMOKE
TEMPERATURE:
200°F

 WOOD PELLETS:
ALDER OR OAK

4 (6-ounce) halibut steaks

¼ cup extra-virgin olive oil

2 teaspoons kosher salt

1 teaspoon freshly ground
black pepper

½ cup mayonnaise

½ cup sweet pickle relish

¼ cup finely chopped
sweet onion

¼ cup chopped roasted
red pepper

¼ cup finely chopped tomato

¼ cup finely chopped
cucumber

2 tablespoons Dijon mustard

1 teaspoon minced garlic

For this recipe, we opt for a premium Dijon mustard over the more common everyday yellow mustard. Why, you ask? Oh, just for the halibut. Ha ha! Seriously, in most of my barbecue recipes that call for mustard, I usually use the cheap yellow variety, because its purpose is more as a spice adherent and it only imparts a light layer of flavor in the final dish. But in this case, the mustard flavor shares the stage with the fish. Think of it as an opportunity to explore the vast world of gourmet mustards that are so trendy right now.

1. Rub the halibut steaks with the olive oil and season on both sides with the salt and pepper. Transfer to a plate, cover with plastic wrap, and refrigerate for 4 hours.

2. Supply your smoker with wood pellets and follow the manufacturer's specific start-up procedure. Preheat, with the lid closed, to 200°F.

3. Remove the halibut from the refrigerator and rub with the mayonnaise.

4. Put the fish directly on the grill grate, close the lid, and smoke for 2 hours, or until opaque and an instant-read thermometer inserted in the fish reads 140°F.

5. While the fish is smoking, combine the pickle relish, onion, roasted red pepper, tomato, cucumber, Dijon mustard, and garlic in a medium bowl. Refrigerate the mustard relish until ready to serve.

6. Serve the halibut steaks hot with the mustard relish.

Substitution Tip This recipe also works great with swordfish or tuna.

CURED COLD-SMOKED LOX

Serves 4 to 6

DRY CURING TIME: 24 HOURS

REFRIGERATION TIME: 24 HOURS

PREP TIME: 20 MINUTES

SMOKE TIME: 6 HOURS

 SMOKE TEMPERATURE: 80°F

 WOOD PELLETS: ALDER

¼ cup salt

¼ cup sugar

1 tablespoon freshly ground black pepper

1 bunch dill, chopped

1 pound sashimi-grade salmon, skin removed

1 avocado, sliced

8 bagels

4 ounces cream cheese

1 bunch alfalfa sprouts

1 (3.5-ounce) jar capers

People pay $30 to $50 a pound for lox, the cured and smoked belly of the salmon, but it's really easy to make at home—and at a third of the cost, why not? You'll need to have the ability to cold-smoke at temperatures lower than many wood pellet grill smokers can sustain without an attachment or accessory like a smoker tube (see Optional Gear on page 10). Be sure to use sashimi-grade salmon, which is safe to eat raw. The dry-curing and cold-smoking process may not kill all bacteria that can occur in salmon, so if you're not using sashimi-grade, you'll need to freeze the salmon for 24 hours before starting to cold-smoke to kill any bacteria.

1. In a small bowl, combine the salt, sugar, pepper, and fresh dill to make the curing mixture. Set aside.

2. On a smooth surface, lay out a large piece of plastic wrap and spread half of the curing salt mixture in the middle, spreading it out to about the size of the salmon.

3. Place the salmon on top of the curing salt.

4. Top the fish with the remaining curing salt, covering it completely. Wrap the salmon, leaving the ends open to drain.

5. Place the wrapped fish in a rimmed baking pan or dish lined with paper towels to soak up liquid.

6. Place a weight on the salmon evenly, such as a pan with a couple of heavy jars of pickles on top.

7. Put the salmon pan with weights in the refrigerator. Place something (a dishtowel, for example) under the back of the pan in order to slightly tip it down so the liquid drains away from the fish.

8. Leave the salmon to cure in the refrigerator for 24 hours.

9. Place the wood pellets in the smoker, but do not follow the start-up procedure and do not preheat.

10. Remove the salmon from the refrigerator, unwrap it, rinse it off, and pat dry.

11. Put the salmon in the smoker while still cold from the refrigerator to slow down the cooking process. You'll need to use a cold-smoker attachment or enlist the help of a smoker tube to hold the temperature at 80°F and maintain that for 6 hours to absorb smoke and complete the cold-smoking process.

12. Remove the salmon from the smoker, place it in a sealed plastic bag, and refrigerate for 24 hours. The salmon will be translucent all the way through.

13. Thinly slice the lox and serve with sliced avocado, bagels, cream cheese, alfalfa sprouts, and capers.

Ingredient Tip There are lots of varieties of smoked salmon, including cured cold-smoked and cooked hot-smoked. But to many people's surprise, real lox is not necessarily smoked. It's just salt-brined.

ROASTED OYSTERS ON THE HALF SHELL WITH COMPOUND BUTTER

Makes 1 dozen

PREP TIME: 20 MINUTES

SMOKE TIME: 15 TO 20 MINUTES

 SMOKE TEMPERATURE: 225°F

 WOOD PELLETS: APPLE, CHERRY, OR OAK

8 tablespoons (1 stick) unsalted butter, at room temperature

¼ cup shredded Parmesan cheese

2 garlic cloves, minced

3 tablespoons chopped fresh parsley

2 tablespoons Worcestershire sauce

2 tablespoons hot sauce

1 teaspoon cayenne pepper

1 dozen raw, shucked oysters in bottom shells; top shells discarded

Where I live, on the coast of South Carolina, oysters are almost considered a party food. But in many places, they have a more revered culinary reputation. Truth is, oysters have been popular at both high-end restaurants and casual joints for years. Believe it or not, oyster stands were once as common in New York City as hot dog carts are now.

1. Supply your smoker with wood pellets and follow the manufacturer's specific start-up procedure. Preheat, with the lid closed, to 225°F.

2. In a small bowl, combine the butter, Parmesan cheese, garlic, parsley, Worcestershire sauce, hot sauce, and cayenne pepper.

3. Top each oyster with 1 tablespoon of the compound butter.

4. Place the oysters in the smoker, close the lid, and smoke for 15 to 20 minutes.

5. Serve immediately with the remaining compound butter.

Ingredient Tip Rustic and irregularly shaped shells can make some oysters difficult to stabilize on the grill grate. Try nesting the shells upon a bed of rock salt (sometimes called ice cream maker salt) in a large cast iron skillet or baking pan.

LEMON-PEPPER BACON SCALLOPS

Serves 4

PREP TIME: 25 TO 30 MINUTES

SMOKE TIME: 25 MINUTES

 SMOKE TEMPERATURE: 225°F

 WOOD PELLETS: CHERRY OR OAK

2 pounds sea scallops (about 20)

8 tablespoons (1 stick) unsalted butter

4 garlic cloves, minced

2 tablespoons freshly squeezed lemon juice

1 tablespoon lemon-pepper seasoning blend

10 slices bacon, cut in half

20 toothpicks, soaked in water for 20 minutes

3 teaspoons chopped fresh basil

Lemon wedges, for serving

Many people say scallops get rubbery on the smoker; you'll need to keep close watch on the internal temperature with an instant-read thermometer so you don't overcook them. Enter bacon! We use very thin-cut bacon (you can even use precooked bacon) to help keep the lean mollusks moist. Bacon is also the duct tape of barbecue. In this recipe, it's almost like gift wrapping. Don't get so excited that you eat the toothpick.

1. Place the scallops on a jelly roll pan (a baking pan with low sides).

2. Supply your smoker with wood pellets and follow the manufacturer's specific start-up procedure. Preheat, with the lid closed, to 225°F.

3. On the stovetop, in a small saucepan over medium-low heat, melt the butter and sauté the garlic in it.

4. Stir in the lemon juice and remove from the heat.

5. Baste the scallops with lemon butter and sprinkle with the lemon-pepper seasoning.

6. Wrap each scallop with a half slice of bacon and secure with toothpicks.

7. Using tongs, gently remove the scallops from the pan and place directly on the grill grate.

8. Close the lid and smoke for 25 minutes, or until opaque and firm with an internal temperature of 130°F.

9. Remove from the heat. Plate the scallops, remove the toothpicks, and sprinkle with the fresh basil.

10. Serve with lemon wedges.

Ingredient Tip Shop for scallops that are as close in size and thickness as possible to ensure even cooking.

LOBSTER TAILS IN GARLIC BUTTER SAUCE

Serves 4

PREP TIME: 30 MINUTES

SMOKE TIME: 45 MINUTES TO 1 HOUR

 SMOKE TEMPERATURE: 225°F

 WOOD PELLETS: OAK

4 (8-ounce) lobster tails, fresh or frozen

1 cup (2 sticks) unsalted butter, melted

¼ cup freshly squeezed lemon juice

1 garlic clove, minced

2 tablespoons chopped fresh parsley, divided

2 teaspoons freshly ground black pepper

1 teaspoon salt

1 teaspoon red pepper flakes

The sight of ruby-red lobster tails on your rugged wood pellet grill is cooler than cool. It's a true feast for the eyes! In fact, very few people have ever experienced wood-smoked lobster. Your guests will feel like royalty. Fun fact: Lobster shells have been used to create the cores of golf balls. But they could never achieve near the distance of modern balls. So, enjoy the buttery richness of the meat, but don't feel guilty throwing out the beautiful shells.

1. Prepare the lobster tails by cutting along the middle of the shell, front to back.

2. Lift the meat from each shell gently, so it rests on the split shell, but be sure to keep it attached at the base of the tail.

3. Make a slit down the center of the meat and place the lobster tails on a perforated pizza pan or Frogmat (or you can smoke directly on the grate).

4. Supply your smoker with wood pellets and follow the manufacturer's specific start-up procedure. Preheat, with the lid closed, to 225°F.

5. In a small bowl, combine the melted butter, lemon juice, garlic, 1 table-spoon of parsley, the pepper, salt, and red pepper flakes.

6. Pour a tablespoon of the butter mixture over each lobster tail.

7. Place the pan on the grill grate (or place the lobster tails directly on the grate), close the lid, and smoke for 1 hour, basting once with the butter mixture, until the meat is white and opaque, with an internal temperature of 130°F to 140°F.

8. Remove the lobster tails from the grill and plate. Sprinkle with the remaining 1 tablespoon of parsley and serve hot with the remaining butter mixture for dipping.

Ingredient Tip Splitting the lobster tail shells allows the delicate meat to smoke more evenly. Hold the tail shell-side up and use kitchen shears to split down to the last shell segment before the tail. Devein and rinse out any grit as needed.

SEASONED TUNA STEAKS

Serves 4

MARINATING TIME: 1 HOUR
PREP TIME: 10 MINUTES
SMOKE TIME: 1 HOUR

 SMOKE
TEMPERATURE:
250°F

 WOOD PELLETS:
OAK

2 tablespoons sesame oil

½ cup soy sauce

Juice of 1 lemon

1 tablespoon minced garlic

1 teaspoon onion powder

1 teaspoon freshly ground
black pepper

1 teaspoon ground ginger

¼ cup chopped scallions

4 (6- to 8-ounce) thick-cut
albacore tuna steaks

Tuna is the most popular fish sold today. But when you own a wood pellet grill smoker, you'll want to think outside of the can. There are at least 15 species of tuna to choose from, but the most common are bluefin, yellowfin, skipjack, and albacore. This recipe calls for a low-and-slow cook to absorb maximum smoke. However, if you're in a hurry, try this one at 450°F for 3 to 10 minutes per side, depending on desired doneness. It is delicious either way, but it just may not absorb as much smoke flavor.

1. In a small bowl, whisk together the sesame oil, soy sauce, lemon juice, minced garlic, onion powder, pepper, ginger, and scallions to make the marinade.

2. Place the tuna steaks in a baking dish. Pour the marinade over them, cover with plastic wrap, and refrigerate for 1 hour only. (If you marinate any longer, the soy sauce will make the tuna too salty.)

3. Supply your smoker with wood pellets and follow the manufacturer's specific start-up procedure. Preheat, with the lid closed, to 250°F.

4. Remove the tuna from the marinade and discard the marinade.

5. Place the tuna steaks directly on the grill grate, close the lid, and smoke for 1 hour, or until the internal temperature registers between 125°F and 145°F, depending on desired doneness.

6. Serve hot.

Pair It Try Southern Slaw (page 156) with this dish.

CREAMY LOWCOUNTRY SHRIMP AND GRITS

Serves 8

PREP TIME: 45 MINUTES

SMOKE TIME: 15 MINUTES

 SMOKE
TEMPERATURE:
450°F

 WOOD PELLETS:
HICKORY

7 cups chicken stock

2 cups water

3 cups white grits

8 tablespoons (1 stick) unsalted butter, divided

4 ounces cream cheese, softened

2 tablespoons minced garlic

2 teaspoons salt, plus more for seasoning

2 teaspoons freshly ground black pepper, plus more for seasoning

1½ pounds tail-off large shrimp, peeled and deveined

¾ cup cream sherry (such as Harveys Bristol Cream Sherry)

1 cup heavy (whipping) cream

1 cup shredded Cheddar cheese

½ cup chopped scallions

Shrimp and grits originated in Charleston, around 1930. Then known as shrimp and hominy, it was cheap to prepare. Now shrimp and grits is a signature Southern dish and there are lots of different variations. Local Charleston writer Nathalie Dupree has filled an entire cookbook with them. Traditional versions typically feature red-eye (coffee-based) gravy, but I prefer the sherry and cream in our smoked version.

1. On the stovetop, in a large pot over high heat, bring the chicken stock and water to a boil.

2. Gradually add the grits to the pot, stirring constantly, to prevent lumps.

3. Cook the grits on low for 25 minutes, then stir in 4 tablespoons of butter, the cream cheese, minced garlic, 2 teaspoons of salt, and 2 teaspoons of pepper.

4. Supply your smoker with wood pellets and follow the manufacturer's specific start-up procedure. Preheat, with the lid closed, to 450°F.

5. Melt the remaining 4 tablespoons of butter in a disposable pan on the grill grate.

6. Season the shrimp with salt and pepper and add to the pan of butter, sautéing for 2 to 3 minutes on each side.

7. Remove the shrimp from the pan but leave the pan on the grill and pour in the cream sherry, stirring until reduced by about half. Add the heavy cream, stirring until thickened.

8. Fold the sherry-cream mixture into the grits.

9. Serve the grits in individual bowls topped with the shrimp, Cheddar cheese, and scallions.

Ingredient Tip Shrimp size is measured by the count of how many shrimp it takes to make a pound. For this recipe, look for large, or 21 to 25 count.

CHARRED SHRIMP SKEWERS

Serves 4

MARINATING TIME: 1 TO 2 HOURS
PREP TIME: 25 MINUTES
SMOKE TIME: 4 TO 6 MINUTES

 SMOKE
TEMPERATURE:
450°F

 WOOD PELLETS:
MESQUITE OR PECAN

1 (13.5-ounce) can
coconut milk

¼ cup rum

1 tablespoon maple syrup

1 tablespoon unsalted butter

¼ cup packed light
brown sugar

1 teaspoon salt

1 teaspoon freshly ground
black pepper

Juice of 1 lime

2 pounds tail-on jumbo shrimp,
peeled and deveined

16 metal or wooden skewers (if
wooden, soaked in water for
30 minutes)

Year after year, shrimp continues to be the most popular seafood in the United States. Being in the Lowcountry (that's the low-lying coastal area of South Carolina), I see shrimp trawlers hard at work on a daily basis. I encourage you to opt for wild shrimp from the Atlantic or South Carolina for this dish. It's good to use a strong-flavored wood pellet like mesquite here since the shrimp cook fast. You need a strong wood that will impart flavor quickly.

1. In a medium bowl, make a marinade by combining the coconut milk, rum, maple syrup, butter, brown sugar, salt, pepper, and lime juice. Blend well. Reserve half of the marinade in another bowl and set aside.

2. Toss the shrimp in the remaining marinade, cover, and refrigerate for 1 to 2 hours.

3. On the stovetop, in a small saucepan over low heat, warm the reserved marinade for about 10 minutes, stirring constantly, until the sauce is reduced and thick and syrupy. Remove from the heat.

4. Supply your smoker with wood pellets and follow the manufacturer's specific start-up procedure. Preheat, with the lid closed, to 450°F.

5. Thread 4 shrimp on each of 8 skewers, then double-skewer with the remaining skewers (see Tip below). Place the skewers directly on the grill grate, baste with the warm sauce, close the lid, and smoke for 2 to 3 minutes, or until pink.

6. Flip the shrimp, baste again, close the lid, and smoke for an additional 2 to 3 minutes.

7. The shrimp will be firm and opaque when fully cooked through—be careful not to overcook them. Remove from the heat and serve immediately.

Technique Tip One trick that keeps skewered items like shrimp from spinning on the stick is to use *two* skewers, or the double-skewer technique. This will make flipping and handling grilled items easier. Flat and wide skewers serve the same purpose, and they're easier than ever to find.

SMOKED PESTO MUSSELS

Serves 2 to 3

SOAKING TIME: 20 MINUTES
PREP TIME: 20 MINUTES
SMOKE TIME: 1 HOUR 30 MINUTES

 SMOKE
TEMPERATURE:
150° TO 180°F
("SMOKE")

 WOOD PELLETS:
ALDER OR CHERRY

1 cup water

1 cup white wine

2 pounds mussels, cleaned and debearded

¾ cup extra-virgin olive oil, divided

½ cup grated Parmesan cheese

¼ cup fresh basil leaves

2 tablespoons pine nuts

1 tablespoon minced garlic

The mussels in this recipe are steamed open on the stovetop and then quickly smoked on the grill for some wood-fire flavor. But if the size of your steaming pot permits, you'll get more smoke when the entire process is completed on the wood pellet grill.

1. On the stovetop, in a large stockpot over medium-high heat, bring the water and wine to a boil, then add one layer of mussels. Steam for 1 to 2 minutes, or until the shells open, then remove the mussels and set aside. Discard any that do not open.

2. Repeat this steaming process until all of the mussels have been steamed open. Strain the liquid and set aside.

3. Remove the mussels from their shells with a knife and place the mussel "meat" back into the liquid to soak for 20 minutes off the heat. The mussels will cool slightly.

4. Meanwhile, in a food processor, pulse ½ cup of olive oil, the Parmesan cheese, basil, pine nuts, and minced garlic until coarsely combined. Store the pesto in the refrigerator until ready to use.

5. Supply your smoker with wood pellets and follow the manufacturer's specific start-up procedure. Preheat, with the lid closed, to 150° to 180°F, or the "Smoke" setting.

6. Place the mussels in a grill basket on the grate, close the lid, and smoke for about 1 hour 30 minutes.

7. Serve the mussels with the pesto.

Pair It Enjoy with the cool and paper plate-bending BLT Pasta Salad (page 159).

SUNDAY SUPPER SALMON WITH OLIVE TAPENADE

Serves 10 to 12

MARINATING TIME: 8 HOURS
TO OVERNIGHT

PREP TIME: 1 HOUR 20 MINUTES

SMOKE TIME: 1 TO 2 HOURS

 SMOKE
TEMPERATURE:
250°F

 WOOD PELLETS:
ALDER

2 cups packed light
brown sugar

½ cup salt

¼ cup maple syrup

⅓ cup crab boil seasoning

1 (3- to 5-pound) whole salmon
fillet, skin removed

¼ cup extra-virgin olive oil

1 (15-ounce) can pitted green
olives, drained

1 (15-ounce) can pitted black
olives, drained

3 tablespoons jarred sun-dried
tomatoes, drained

3 tablespoons chopped
fresh basil

1 tablespoon dried oregano

2 tablespoons freshly squeezed
lemon juice

2 tablespoons jarred
capers, drained

2 tablespoons chopped fresh
parsley, plus more for sprinkling

Planks for the memories. You can make this grilled salmon feast even more memorable by adding an aromatic layer of cedar smoke. Prior to cooking, soak your cedar plank for at least two hours in water to add steaming moisture to the fish. The indirect heat and low-and-slow smoke should keep the planks from catching fire.

1. In a medium bowl, combine the brown sugar, salt, maple syrup, and crab boil seasoning.

2. Rub the paste all over the salmon and place the fish in a shallow dish. Cover and marinate in the refrigerator for at least 8 hours or overnight.

3. Remove the salmon from dish, rinse, pat dry, and let stand for 1 hour to take off the chill.

4. Meanwhile, in a food processor, pulse the olive oil, green olives, black olives, sun-dried tomatoes, basil, oregano, lemon juice, capers, and parsley to a chunky consistency. Refrigerate the tapenade until ready to serve.

5. Supply your smoker with wood pellets and follow the manufacturer's specific start-up procedure. Preheat, with the lid closed, to 250°F.

6. Place the salmon on the grill grate (or on a cedar plank on the grill grate), close the lid, and smoke for 1 to 2 hours, or until the internal temperature reaches 140°F to 145°F. When the fish flakes easily with a fork, it's done.

7. Remove the salmon from the heat and sprinkle with parsley. Serve with the olive tapenade.

Smoking Tip Custom-cut and expensive cedar planks are not required here. You can save a few bucks and use untreated natural cedar roofing shingles from your nearest home superstore. Just be sure to wash them first.

SUMMER PAELLA

Serves 8

PREP TIME: 1 HOUR

SMOKE TIME: 45 MINUTES

 SMOKE
TEMPERATURE:
450°F

 WOOD PELLETS:
ALDER OR OAK

6 tablespoons extra-virgin olive oil, divided, plus more for drizzling

2 green or red bell peppers, cored, seeded, and diced

2 medium onions, diced

2 garlic cloves, slivered

1 (29-ounce) can tomato purée

1½ pounds chicken thighs

Kosher salt

1½ pounds tail-on shrimp, peeled and deveined

1 cup dried thinly sliced chorizo sausage

1 tablespoon smoked paprika

1½ teaspoons saffron threads

2 quarts chicken broth

3½ cups white rice

2 (7½-ounce) cans chipotle chiles in adobo sauce

1½ pounds fresh clams, soaked in cold water for 15 to 20 minutes

2 tablespoons chopped fresh parsley

2 lemons, cut into wedges, for serving

My memories of paella don't trace back to early Spain; they start with a classic 1994 *Seinfeld* episode. Kramer called it an orgiastic feast for the senses, and I still don't know what that means. But I do know that paella is the ultimate one-pan dish for the backyard barbecue. Thanks to the steady temperature of your wood pellet grill, the process has never been easier to tackle at home. If you don't own a thin carbon-steel paella pan, feel free to use a large stainless-steel or aluminum skillet. Cast iron and nonstick pans are discouraged for paella.

1. Make the sofrito: On the stovetop, in a saucepan over medium-low heat, combine ¼ cup of olive oil, the bell peppers, onions, and garlic, and cook for 5 minutes, or until the onions are translucent.

2. Stir in the tomato purée, reduce the heat to low, and simmer, stirring frequently, until most of the liquid has evaporated, about 30 minutes. Set aside. (Note: The sofrito can be made in advance and refrigerated.)

3. Supply your smoker with wood pellets and follow the manufacturer's specific start-up procedure. Preheat, with the lid closed, to 450°F.

4. Heat a large paella pan on the smoker and add the remaining 2 table-spoons of olive oil.

5. Add the chicken thighs, season lightly with salt, and brown for 6 to 10 minutes, then push to the outer edge of the pan.

6. Add the shrimp, season with salt, close the lid, and smoke for 3 minutes.

7. Add the sofrito, chorizo, paprika, and saffron, and stir together.

8. In a separate bowl, combine the chicken broth, uncooked rice, and 1 tablespoon of salt, stirring until well combined.

9. Add the broth-rice mixture to the paella pan, spreading it evenly over the other ingredients.

10. Close the lid and smoke for 5 minutes, then add the chipotle chiles and clams on top of the rice.

11. Close the lid and continue to smoke the paella for about 30 minutes, or until all of the liquid is absorbed.

12. Remove the pan from the grill, cover tightly with aluminum foil, and let rest off the heat for 5 minutes.

13. Drizzle with olive oil, sprinkle with the fresh parsley, and serve with the lemon wedges.

Ingredient Tip Sofrito is a Spanish tomato sauce, usually made with olive oil, onions, peppers, and garlic. It's used as a base for many dishes. Variations of the original have spread throughout Latin America, Europe, and the world.

Chapter 7

OTHER MEATS YOU CAN SMOKE

There's more to barbecue than just ribs, chicken, burgers, and brisket. Wood pellet grills make low and slow so easy, it's understandable that you may want to stick with what you know. But because your grill can also maintain 425°F just as easily as a steady 180°F, your options are almost endless. If you're a hunter, here is where you can pick up a few ideas for how to infuse smoke into pheasant, venison, and quail. If you're not a hunter but want to purchase wild or farmed game, just check with your nearest wild game processor or taxidermist. They often offer fresh or frozen meats for sale in-store, or they will happily point you to the nearest market. If you want to branch out to other mainstream regional specialties, check out the leg of lamb, kielbasa, and gyro recipes later in this chapter. Plus, you really need to try homemade jerky and smoking a fatty (it's probably *not* what you think). Read on! ◊

◀ BISON BURGERS, page 128

THE NAME GAME

Deer hunters have a great tool in the wood pellet smoker. In culinary terms, **venison** is meat from deer, elk, moose, caribou, antelope, and pronghorn. If you are purchasing packaged venison, the name of the specific animal must be listed on the package label.

Lamb and **mutton** are often misunderstood, but the difference is simple: Lamb is younger than about a year old; mutton is older. Mutton isn't as popular as it used to be for general consumption.

Cornish game hens have a name more exotic than what they really are—not wild game at all but simply a breed of chicken. Also called Rock Cornish, or poussin, these "hens" are male or female broiler chickens, less than five weeks old. They taste like chicken but are smaller birds. It almost seems like Cornish game hens have been around forever, but they were actually first bred in the 1950s. Fun fact: The late funny man and musician Victor Borge was an early investor and promoter who helped make the dish common.

A **fatty** is basically a smoked meatloaf, and it is relatively new to the barbecue world, with infinite variations. It came to the forefront a few years ago when a bacon-weave-wrapped fatty dubbed the "bacon explosion" went viral as an Internet oddity.

WILD AND FARMED GAME

Hunters and friends of hunters know that game meats from deer to quail taste even better with the addition of wood smoke. Look around and you'll find local markets and sources from which to purchase both wild game and farm-raised game. Game is simply any animal that is hunted for sport or food. Thus, the animals available vary by country and culture.

It is legal to sell wild game, but it must be inspected. Every inspected meat product is required to be packaged with a label indicating the agency that inspected the meat. The label will have a small logo shaped like a triangle or circle, or even a special one with a number identifying the processing establishment. If the packaging and label *do not* display such a mark, this means the meat was not inspected. If they *do* have this mark, then it should be legal to sell.

The meat of farm-raised game animals has a stronger flavor than that of domesticated animals, yet it is *milder* than wild game meat. The factors that determine the meat's overall quality include the age of the animal (younger animals are more tender), what the animal ate, and the season it was killed. Fall is considered the best time to buy farm-raised meat thanks to the abundant feeding that takes place in the summer.

Game Flavor-Saver

To minimize gamy flavors in wild meats like venison, elk, and boar, remove all fat and silverskin and eliminate excess blood. Soak the meat overnight in a buttermilk solution with salt or vinegar and sugar or other spices as desired.

Salt solution: 1 tablespoon per quart of cold water.

Vinegar solution: 1 cup per quart of cold water.

Use enough solution to cover the game completely. Discard the solution after soaking.

Game bird meat is darker (and has more umami-flavor "gaminess") than domestic poultry, but it is still considered white meat. The meat is darker because more oxygen is needed by the wild bird's muscles and therefore, it has more red blood cells. This is true of farm-raised birds to a lesser degree, based on the animal's activity.

All game mammals are considered red meat. The protein myoglobin holds oxygen in the muscles and gives the meat a darker color.

RULES TO GRILL BY

When you veer off the basic barbecue path, keep these tips in mind for best success:

★ Lean meats call for marinades and moisture. Place water pans in with your meats to promote moist heat circulation in your smoker.

★ Other ways to boost moisture include basting, larding (inserting slivers of fat in the meat), and barding (wrapping the meat in fat, such as bacon).

★ Think local. Head to your farmers' market and ask around to find locally grown meats or a special breed of pork to try in your wood pellet grill. Local venison may be the perfect excuse to try making Venison Steaks (page 144).

★ Certain animals won't be helped by smoke. Avoid sea ducks and fowl that you might suspect are fish eaters.

★ Never smoke unplucked fowl.

BISON BURGERS

Serves 6

PREP TIME: 25 TO 30 MINUTES

SMOKE TIME: 17 TO 19 MINUTES

 SMOKE
TEMPERATURE:
425°F

 WOOD PELLETS:
MESQUITE OR
BBQ BLEND

2 pounds ground bison

2 tablespoons steak seasoning

4 tablespoons (½ stick)
unsalted butter, cut into pieces

1 large onion, finely minced

6 slices Swiss cheese

6 ciabatta buns, split

Sweet and Spicy Jalapeño
Relish (page 192), for serving

Lettuce and sliced tomatoes,
for serving

Did you know buffalo and bison are actually two different animals? It's true. Early American explorers mistakenly referred to bison as buffalo because the animals resembled Old World buffalo, but they are really a separate species. Here in the States, what you may have heard called buffalo meat is really the meat of a bison. Bison burgers offer a leaner, healthier alternative to ground beef burgers.

1. Supply your smoker with wood pellets and follow the manufacturer's specific start-up procedure. Preheat, with the lid closed, to 425°F.

2. In a large bowl, combine the ground bison and steak seasoning until well blended.

3. Shape the meat mixture into 6 patties and make a thumb indentation in the center of each. Set aside.

4. Place a rimmed baking sheet on the grill and add the butter and onion. Sauté for 5 minutes, or until the onion is translucent. Top with the bison burger patties, indention-side down.

5. Close the lid and smoke for 6 to 7 minutes, then flip the burgers and smother them in the sautéed onion. Close the lid again and continue smoking for 6 to 7 minutes. During the last few minutes of cooking, top each burger with a slice of Swiss cheese. For safe consumption, the internal temperature should reach between 140°F (medium) and 160°F (well-done).

6. Lightly toast the ciabatta buns, split-side down, on one side of the smoker.

7. Serve the onion-smothered cheeseburgers on the toasted buns with jalapeño relish, lettuce, and tomato—or whatever toppings you like.

Pair It For a kicked-up game burger, try adding Smoked Goose Bacon (page 133) on top!

CHORIZO QUESO FUNDIDO

Serves 4 to 6

PREP TIME: 40 TO 45 MINUTES

SMOKE TIME: 20 TO 25 MINUTES

 SMOKE
TEMPERATURE:
350°F

 WOOD PELLETS:
APPLE

1 poblano chile

1 cup chopped queso
quesadilla or queso Oaxaca

1 cup shredded Monterey
Jack cheese

¼ cup milk

1 tablespoon all-purpose flour

2 (4-ounce) links
Mexican chorizo sausage,
casings removed

⅓ cup beer

1 tablespoon unsalted butter

1 small red onion, chopped

½ cup whole kernel corn

2 serrano chiles or jalapeño
peppers, stemmed, seeded,
and coarsely chopped

1 tablespoon minced garlic

1 tablespoon freshly squeezed
lime juice

1 teaspoon ground cumin

1 teaspoon salt

1 teaspoon freshly ground
black pepper

1 tablespoon chopped fresh
cilantro

1 tablespoon chopped scallions

Tortilla chips, for serving

Mexican chorizo is a raw hot sausage that is typically used for Mexican-American dishes like dips, eggs, and tacos. It's different from Spanish chorizo, which is a cured sausage that's more likely to be found with dried sausage and salami. We use the fresh Mexican chorizo in this recipe, and we add it in at the end for a pop of color and signature flavor. Queso fundido is akin to fondue: It's an ooey-gooey, cheesy dip to enjoy with nacho chips.

1. Supply your smoker with wood pellets and follow the manufacturer's specific start-up procedure. Preheat, with the lid closed, to 350°F.

2. On the smoker or over medium-high heat on the stovetop, place the poblano directly on the grate (or burner) to char for 1 to 2 minutes, turning as needed. Remove from heat and place in a closed-up lunch-size paper bag for 2 minutes to sweat and further loosen the skin.

3. Remove the skin and coarsely chop the poblano, removing the seeds; set aside.

4. In a bowl, combine the queso quesadilla, Monterey Jack, milk, and flour; set aside.

5. On the stovetop, in a cast iron skillet over medium heat, cook and crumble the chorizo for about 2 minutes.

6. Transfer the cooked chorizo to a small, grill-safe pan and place over indirect heat on the smoker.

7. Place the cast iron skillet on the preheated grill grate. Pour in the beer and simmer for a few minutes, loosening and stirring in any remaining sausage bits from the pan.

8. Add the butter to the pan, then add the cheese mixture a little at a time, stirring constantly.

CONTINUED

9. When the cheese is smooth, stir in the onion, corn, serrano chiles, garlic, lime juice, cuvmin, salt, and pepper. Stir in the reserved chopped charred poblano.

10. Close the lid and smoke for 15 to 20 minutes to infuse the queso with smoke flavor and further cook the vegetables.

11. When the cheese is bubbly, top with the chorizo mixture and garnish with the cilantro and scallions.

12. Serve the chorizo queso fundido hot with tortilla chips.

Ingredient Tip Try using leftover grilled corn cut from the cob for better texture and added smoke flavor.

CORNISH GAME HEN

Serves 4

PREP TIME: 10 MINUTES

SMOKE TIME: 2 TO 3 HOURS

 SMOKE
TEMPERATURE:
275°F

 WOOD PELLETS:
APPLE OR BOURBON
BROWN SUGAR BLEND

4 Cornish game hens

Extra-virgin olive oil,
for rubbing

2 teaspoons salt

1 teaspoon freshly ground
black pepper

1 teaspoon celery seeds

Cornish game hens have become my favorite food for impressing guests. First, the game hen sounds way more exotic than it is (it's really just a chicken). Second, these birds are readily available at most supermarkets. Finally, each plate is a feast for the eyes because everyone gets their own bird! Plus, there's no fighting over drumsticks.

1. Supply your smoker with wood pellets and follow the manufacturer's specific start-up procedure. Preheat, with the lid closed, to 275°F.

2. Rub the game hens over and under the skin with olive oil and season all over with the salt, pepper, and celery seeds.

3. Place the birds directly on the grill grate, close the lid, and smoke for 2 to 3 hours, or until a meat thermometer inserted in each bird reads 170°F.

4. Serve the Cornish game hens hot.

Pair It Serve with S'mores Dip Skillet (page 172) for dessert.

ITALIAN FATTY

Serves 4

PREP TIME: 20 MINUTES

SMOKE TIME: 2 HOURS

 SMOKE
TEMPERATURE:
225°F

 WOOD PELLETS:
OAK

1 pound ground sausage

2 teaspoons salt, plus more for seasoning

2 teaspoons freshly ground black pepper, plus more for seasoning

1 pound bacon

8 thin slices ham

8 slices Swiss cheese

2 tomatoes, thinly sliced

¼ cup sliced pepperoncini

2 teaspoons chopped fresh oregano

2 teaspoons chopped fresh basil

1 teaspoon garlic powder

Splash of canola oil

Splash of balsamic vinegar

Shout out to my Carolina pit master pal Jack Waiboer, who devised this recipe with the most brilliant shortcut of all time. He suggests heading to your favorite sub shop and ordering a large Italian sub "deconstructed." In other words, bag up all the meat, cheese, and toppings separately, and take home the sub roll uncut for a later use. They'll even season your veggies in a baggie with the oil and spices! Add a pack of bacon and one sausage chub (that's what they call those one-pound sausage tubes in the store). You'll have everything you need to create this fat Italian masterpiece.

1. Supply your smoker with wood pellets and follow the manufacturer's specific start-up procedure. Preheat, with the lid closed, to 225°F.

2. Season the ground sausage with the salt and pepper, blending well.

3. On a flat surface, vertically lay out half of the bacon strips side by side. Layer horizontally with the remaining bacon strips in an under-over pattern, creating a tight weave.

4. Spread the ground sausage over the bacon to completely cover it.

5. Layer the ham slices on top of the ground sausage, then layer on the cheese slices and the tomato slices.

6. Sprinkle the pepperoncini slices over the tomato slices and season with the oregano, basil, and garlic powder, and salt and pepper to taste.

7. Drizzle the fatty with a splash of canola oil and balsamic vinegar.

8. Starting from one side, roll the fatty up tightly and tuck in the bacon weave to secure.

9. Place the bacon-wrapped fatty on the smoker seam-side down. Close the lid and smoke for about 2 hours, or until a meat thermometer inserted into the sausage meat reads 160°F.

10. Slice the fatty and serve.

Smoking Tip Bacon weaves can be a slippery mess to put together. Be sure to start with cold ingredients and construct your weave on top of a sheet of plastic wrap to make handling—and especially rolling—your fatty easier.

SMOKED GOOSE BACON

Serves 8

INITIAL BRINING TIME: OVERNIGHT

CHILL TIME (AFTER FIRST
SMOKE): 1 HOUR IN THE
FREEZER TO AID IN SLICING

MARINATING TIME (AFTER
SLICING): 1 HOUR

PREP TIME: 30 MINUTES

SMOKE TIME: 4 HOURS 15 MINUTES

 SMOKE
TEMPERATURE:
165°F, 250°F

 WOOD PELLETS:
CHERRY

FOR THE BRINE

4 cups hot water

2 cups freshly brewed
hot coffee

1 cup salt

1 cup packed brown sugar

2 goose breasts

FOR THE GOOSE BACON

½ cup soy sauce

½ cup packed brown sugar

1 tablespoon garlic powder

1 tablespoon onion powder

1 tablespoon Sriracha

Ready to get your goose on? This may seem like a complicated recipe, but it's not—although, like all good barbecue it *does* take time. You've got to smoke it twice, but it's worth it. This is the best way to cook your goose!

TO MAKE THE BRINE

1. In a large container with a lid, combine the hot water, hot coffee, salt, and brown sugar, and stir until the salt and sugar are dissolved.

2. Let the brine cool, then add the goose breasts to the container, cover, and refrigerate overnight.

TO MAKE THE GOOSE BACON

1. Remove the goose breasts from the brine, rinse off, and pat dry. Discard the brine.

2. Supply your smoker with wood pellets and follow the manufacturer's specific start-up procedure. Preheat, with the lid closed, to 165°F.

3. Place the goose breasts directly on the grill, close the lid, and smoke the breasts for 3 hours. When finished, let cool, then transfer to a container with a lid, cover, and freeze for 1 hour to aid in slicing.

4. In a medium bowl, combine the soy sauce, brown sugar, garlic powder, onion powder, and Sriracha.

5. Slice the well-chilled goose breasts thinly against the grain and place the slices in the soy sauce mixture. Cover with plastic wrap and transfer the bowl to the refrigerator to marinate for 1 hour.

6. Supply your smoker with more wood pellets, if necessary, and follow the manufacturer's start-up procedure. Preheat, with the lid closed, to 250°F.

7. Arrange the bacon slices directly on the grill grate, close the lid, and smoke for 1 hour and 15 minutes, turning once.

8. Let the bacon cool slightly and serve warm.

Smoking Tip Don't skip the brining process at the beginning. Goose is a very lean meat, so you need the brine for flavor and to help retain moisture during smoking.

BEEF JERKY

Makes about 20 slices

MARINATING TIME: OVERNIGHT
PREP TIME: 10 MINUTES
SMOKE TIME: 4 TO 5 HOURS

 SMOKE
TEMPERATURE:
150° TO 180°F
("SMOKE")

 WOOD PELLETS:
HICKORY OR PECAN

2 pounds flank steak or bottom round, chilled to almost frozen

1 tablespoon celery salt

1 tablespoon celery seeds

½ cup soy sauce

¼ cup brewed coffee

¼ cup Worcestershire sauce

2 teaspoons garlic powder

2 teaspoons freshly ground black pepper

Dehydrating beef to make jerky was first devised as a popular method for preserving meat. These days, jerky is also popular as a protein-packed snack and travel food. Though it's far from being health food, jerky allows for a lot of sustenance in a tiny, portable package. Plus, it's popular with backpackers, in military rations, and as astronaut space food. So when you're carrying jerky, you know you're one of the cool kids.

1. Cut the beef against the grain into ¼-inch-thick strips.

2. Evenly rub the meat on both sides with the celery salt and celery seeds.

3. In a large bowl, whisk together the soy sauce, coffee, Worcestershire sauce, garlic powder, and pepper.

4. Add the beef to the marinade, cover tightly, and refrigerate overnight.

5. Supply your smoker with wood pellets and follow the manufacturer's specific start-up procedure. Preheat, with the lid closed, to 150° to 180°F, or the "Smoke" setting.

6. Remove the meat from the marinade and blot dry with paper towels, but do not rinse. Discard the marinade.

7. Arrange the meat slices in a single layer on the grill grate, close the lid, and smoke for 4 to 5 hours, or until dry yet pliable, with a dark-brown sheen.

8. Let the jerky cool and refrigerate in an airtight container for up to 3 weeks.

Ingredient Tip Store-bought snack-meat sticks and jerky are loaded with artificial nitrites, which are used for curing and to create the reddish-brown color. Celery is a natural source of nitrates, plus I love the taste. That's why early in the prep I have you rub in plenty.

SMOKED PHEASANT

Serves 4 to 6

BRINING TIME: 8 TO 12 HOURS
PREP TIME: 25 MINUTES
SMOKE TIME: 3 TO 4 HOURS

 SMOKE
TEMPERATURE:
250°F

 WOOD PELLETS:
APPLE, CHERRY,
OR HICKORY

1 gallon hot water

1 cup salt

1 cup packed brown sugar

2 (2- to 3-pound) whole
pheasants, cleaned
and plucked

¼ cup extra-virgin olive oil

2 tablespoons onion powder

2 tablespoons freshly ground
black pepper

2 tablespoons cayenne pepper

1 tablespoon minced garlic

2 teaspoons smoked paprika

1 cup molasses

A feast of pheasant has long been considered a delicacy, not only in America but also worldwide. In fact, pheasant hunting is popular in just about every part of the United States, but it is especially popular in the Great Plains. Like me, pheasants are officially omnivores (but they eat a lot more seeds and bugs than I do). Wild pheasants are typically smaller than farm-raised birds. They cook quicker, so adjust the grill time accordingly.

1. In a large container with a lid, combine the hot water, salt, and brown sugar, stirring to dissolve the salt and sugar. Let cool to room temperature, then submerge the pheasants in the brine, cover, and refrigerate for 8 to 12 hours.

2. Remove the pheasants from the brine, then rinse them and pat dry. Discard the brine.

3. Supply your smoker with wood pellets and follow the manufacturer's specific start-up procedure. Preheat, with the lid closed, to 250°F.

4. In a small bowl, combine the olive oil, black pepper, cayenne pepper, onion powder, garlic, and paprika to form a paste.

5. Rub the pheasants with the paste and place breast-side up on the grill grate. Close the lid and smoke for 1 hour.

6. Open the smoker and baste the pheasants with some of the molasses. Close the lid and continue smoking for 2 to 3 hours, basting with the molasses every 30 minutes, until a meat thermometer inserted into the thigh reads 160°F.

7. Remove the pheasants from the grill and let rest for 20 minutes before serving warm or cold.

Pair It Try this dish with the hearty Potluck Salad with Smoked Cornbread (page 160).

SUCCULENT LAMB CHOPS

Serves 3 to 4

MARINATING TIME: 2 HOURS
PREP TIME: 15 MINUTES
SMOKE TIME: 10 TO 20 MINUTES

 SMOKE
TEMPERATURE:
165°F, 450°F

 WOOD PELLETS:
CHERRY

FOR THE MARINADE

½ cup rice wine vinegar

1 teaspoon liquid smoke

2 tablespoons extra-virgin olive oil

2 tablespoons dried minced onion

1 tablespoon chopped fresh mint

FOR THE LAMB CHOPS

8 (4-ounce) lamb chops

½ cup hot pepper jelly

1 tablespoon Sriracha

1 teaspoon salt

1 teaspoon freshly ground black pepper

Lamb chops are underrated by barbecue fans. The fatty, bone-in succulence is perfect for the licking flames of a high-heat grill. It's preferable for lamb to be on the medium-rare side; to achieve that with your pellet smoker, start your grill out low and slow, and wait until the end of your cook to give the chops a high-temperature "reverse" sear. You can use pricier rib lamb chops for this recipe, but I prefer little loin chops. They are a bit meatier, with the same great flavor, and you get extra points because they look like tiny T-bone steaks.

TO MAKE THE MARINADE

In a small bowl, whisk together the rice wine vinegar, liquid smoke, olive oil, minced onion, and mint.

TO MAKE THE LAMB CHOPS

1. Place the lamb chops in an aluminum roasting pan. Pour the marinade over the meat, turning to coat thoroughly. Cover with plastic wrap and marinate in the refrigerator for 2 hours.

2. Supply your smoker with wood pellets and follow the manufacturer's specific start-up procedure. Preheat, with the lid closed, to 165°F, or the "Smoke" setting.

3. On the stovetop, in a small saucepan over low heat, combine the hot pepper jelly and Sriracha and keep warm.

4. When ready to cook the chops, remove them from the marinade and pat dry. Discard the marinade.

5. Season the chops with the salt and pepper, then place them directly on the grill grate, close the lid, and smoke for 5 minutes to "breathe" some smoke into them.

6. Remove the chops from the grill. Increase the pellet cooker temperature to 450°F, or the "High" setting. Once the grill is up to temperature, place the chops on the grill and sear, cooking for 2 minutes per side to achieve medium-rare chops. A meat thermometer inserted in the thickest part of the meat should read 145°F. Continue grilling, if necessary, to your desired doneness.

7. Serve the chops with the warm Sriracha pepper jelly on the side.

Ingredient Tip Shop for grass-fed lamb for the best flavor, and balance the fatty richness by experimenting with acids such as vinegar and lemon juice in your marinade.

POLISH KIELBASA

Serves 8

REFRIGERATING TIME:
8 HOURS TO OVERNIGHT

PREP TIME: 45 MINUTES TO 1 HOUR

SMOKE TIME: 1 HOUR 30 MINUTES
TO 2 HOURS

 SMOKE
TEMPERATURE:
225°F

 WOOD PELLETS: OAK,
PECAN, OR HICKORY

4 pounds ground pork

½ cup water

2 garlic cloves, minced

4 teaspoons salt

1 teaspoon freshly ground
black pepper

1 teaspoon dried marjoram

½ teaspoon ground allspice

14 feet natural hog casings,
medium size

Making sausage from scratch can be a lot of fun. If you're making links, as you will be with this kielbasa, you'll need to make a decision about the proper casing. Your choice is between natural or synthetic. I recommend natural casings, which come from the intestines of hogs or other animals and are known to give sausage a telltale snap with every bite. Medium casings are 32 to 35mm (1¼ to 1⅛ inches), and large casings are 35 to 44mm (1⅛ to 1¾ inches). Medium casings are a good choice for this recipe.

1. In a large bowl, combine the pork, water, garlic, salt, pepper, marjoram, and allspice.

2. Stuff the casings according to the instructions on your sausage stuffing device, or use a funnel (see Tip).

3. Twist the casings according to your desired length and prick each with a pin in several places so the kielbasa won't burst.

4. Transfer the kielbasa to a plate, cover with plastic wrap, and refrigerate for at least 8 hours or overnight.

5. Remove from the refrigerator and allow the links to come to room temperature.

6. Supply your smoker with wood pellets and follow the manufacturer's specific start-up procedure. Preheat, with the lid closed, to 225°F.

7. Place the kielbasa directly on the grill grate, close the lid, and smoke for 1 hour 30 minutes to 2 hours, or until a meat thermometer inserted in each link reads 155°F. (The internal temperature will rise about 5°F when resting, for a finished temp of 160°F.)

8. Serve with buns and condiments of your choosing, or cut up the kielbasa and serve with smoked cabbage (from Corned Beef and Cabbage, page 88).

Technique Tip Stuffing sausage casings is made easier by enlisting the help of a mechanical sausage stuffer. KitchenAid even makes a grinding and stuffing attachment for their famous stand mixers. Run water through the casing to rinse and then slip the open end over the tip of the stuffer or funnel. Push the casing up over the tip, leaving only two inches remaining, and tie off the end. Using your stuffing device or your fingers, push the ground sausage slowly into the casing, being careful not to overfill and break the casing. You can watch me go through the process at www.BarbecueTricks. com/home-made-brats-and-sausage.

GRILLED LASAGNA

Serves 10 to 12

PREP TIME: 1 HOUR

SMOKE TIME: 45 TO 50 MINUTES

 SMOKE TEMPERATURE: 375°F

 WOOD PELLETS: HICKORY

½ pound ground beef

½ pound ground pork sausage

1 medium onion, diced

1 bell pepper, diced

1 tablespoon minced garlic

1 tablespoon dried basil

1 tablespoon dried oregano

1 (15-ounce) can tomato sauce

2 (14.5-ounce) cans diced tomatoes with their juices

15 ounces ricotta cheese

3 cups shredded mozzarella cheese, divided

½ cup grated Parmesan cheese

1 egg, beaten

Nonstick cooking spray

1 (16-ounce) package dry lasagna noodles

For years, they said, "Pasta on the grill just isn't possible!" I'm still working on keeping spaghetti from falling through the grates, but I've mastered lasagna—it's smokable. Now you can infuse that wonderful smoke essence into a dish that's already layered with flavor. The secret weapon is your pellet cooker's ability to maintain baking temperatures. You'll need a 3-quart aluminum pan, or two smaller pans.

1. On the stovetop, in a skillet over medium-high heat, cook the ground beef and ground pork sausage for 5 to 7 minutes, or until browned. Break it up into crumbles.

2. Remove from the heat, drain off the fat from the skillet, and stir in the onion, bell pepper, garlic, basil, oregano, tomato sauce, and diced tomatoes and their juices.

3. Supply your smoker with wood pellets and follow the manufacturer's specific start-up procedure. Preheat, with the lid closed, to 375°F.

4. In a medium bowl, combine the ricotta, 1 cup of mozzarella, the Parmesan, and egg.

5. Spray a 3-quart aluminum pan with cooking spray and spread ½ cup of the meat sauce mixture in the bottom of the pan to cover.

6. Dip the lasagna noodles in water to soften slightly.

7. In the pan, layer one-third of the noodles over the sauce and cover with another ½ cup of sauce.

8. Continue layering in this order: 1 cup of ricotta cheese mixture, 1 cup of sauce, ½ cup of mozzarella, another one-third of the noodles, the remaining ricotta cheese mixture, 1 cup of sauce, ½ cup of mozzarella, the remaining noodles, and then top with the remaining sauce.

9. Cover the pan with aluminum foil and bake on the grill, with the lid closed, for 30 minutes.

10. Remove the foil, top the lasagna with the remaining 1 cup of mozzarella, and continue grilling with the lid closed for 15 to 20 minutes, or until bubbly.

11. Let the lasagna rest for 15 minutes prior to serving.

Smoking Tip If you like plumper pasta, feel free to boil your lasagna noodles in advance, but I suggest skipping that and saving the time and energy. A quick dip in water along with the moisture from the sauce is enough to soften typical dry boxed lasagna noodles.

SMOKED CHRISTMAS CROWN ROAST OF LAMB

Serves 4

PREP TIME: 1 HOUR

SMOKE TIME: 1 HOUR 30 MINUTES
TO 2 HOURS

 SMOKE
TEMPERATURE:
275°F

 WOOD PELLETS:
APPLE, CHERRY,
OR OAK

2 racks of lamb, trimmed,
frenched, and tied into a crown

1¼ cups extra-virgin olive
oil, divided

2 tablespoons chopped
fresh basil

2 tablespoons chopped fresh
rosemary

2 tablespoons ground sage

2 tablespoons ground thyme

8 garlic cloves, minced

2 teaspoons salt

2 teaspoons freshly ground
black pepper

I like to imagine that the crown roast comes from one rack of ribs. In reality, that double-length dachshund lamb would look a little freaky. You'll need to purchase two bone-in racks of lamb and have your butcher trim and french them, then tie them into a crown. Frenching is the process of removing the meat between each bone using a small knife, so that 1½ inch of bone is exposed at the end.

1. Set the lamb out on the counter to take the chill off, about an hour.

2. In a small bowl, combine 1 cup of olive oil, the basil, rosemary, sage, thyme, garlic, salt, and pepper.

3. Baste the entire crown with the herbed olive oil and wrap the exposed frenched bones in aluminum foil.

4. Supply your smoker with wood pellets and follow the manufacturer's specific start-up procedure. Preheat, with the lid closed, to 275°F.

5. Put the lamb directly on the grill, close the lid, and smoke for 1 hour 30 minutes to 2 hours, or until a meat thermometer inserted in the thickest part reads 140°F.

6. Remove the lamb from the heat, tent with foil, and let rest for about 15 minutes before serving. The temperature will rise about 5°F during the rest period, for a finished temperature of 145°F.

Technique Tip The "guard of honor" style is another super regal way to present your lamb. Tie the two racks side to side, with the bones arching inward and crossing like the rifles of an honor guard. And yes, people will laugh if you cap the bones with little white paper booties.

SPATCHCOCKED QUAIL WITH SMOKED FRUIT

Serves 4

PREP TIME: 20 MINUTES
SMOKE TIME: 1 HOUR

 SMOKE
TEMPERATURE:
225°F

 WOOD PELLETS:
HICKORY

4 quail, spatchcocked

2 teaspoons salt

2 teaspoons freshly ground
black pepper

2 teaspoons garlic powder

4 ripe peaches or pears

4 tablespoons (½ stick) salted
butter, softened

1 tablespoon sugar

1 teaspoon ground cinnamon

Spatchcocking is a funny term for butterflying, as described in chapter 3 (see page 41). It's the same technique for quail as it is for turkey and chicken, but you are simply removing the spine of a smaller bird. If you need help with this, you can ask your butcher to do it for you. Smoking the spatchcocked quail under a foil-wrapped brick flattens it and promotes more even cooking.

1. Supply your smoker with wood pellets and follow the manufacturer's specific start-up procedure. Preheat, with the lid closed, to 225°F.

2. Season the quail all over with the salt, pepper, and garlic powder.

3. Cut the peaches (or pears) in half and remove the pits (or the cores).

4. In a small bowl, combine the butter, sugar, and cinnamon; set aside.

5. Arrange the quail on the grill grate, close the lid, and smoke for about 1 hour, or until a meat thermometer inserted in the thickest part reads 145°F.

6. After the quail has been cooking for about 15 minutes, add the peaches (or pears) to the grill, flesh-side down, and smoke for 30 to 40 minutes.

7. Top the cooked peaches (or pears) with the cinnamon butter and serve alongside the quail.

Pair It   To complete the meal, serve with Brussels Sprout Bites with Cilantro-Balsamic Drizzle (page 155).

YUMMY GYRO

Serves 4 to 6

MARINATING TIME: OVERNIGHT
PREP TIME: 25 MINUTES
SMOKE TIME: 35-40 MINUTES

 SMOKE
TEMPERATURE:
300°F, 450°F

 WOOD PELLETS:
APPLE OR CHERRY

1 pound ground lamb

2 teaspoons salt

1 teaspoon freshly ground
black pepper

2 tablespoons chopped
fresh oregano

1 tablespoon minced garlic

1 tablespoon onion powder

4 to 6 pocketless pitas

Tzatziki sauce, for serving

1 tomato, chopped, for serving

1 small onion, thinly sliced,
for serving

My first real job as a teenager was in a suburban Chicago deli called Spiro's, in Glenview, Illinois. They still serve the style of gyro that I consider perfection. The meat is hand-carved off of fire extinguisher-size cones that are slow roasting in vertical rotisseries. This allows for plenty of crispy brown bark in each sandwich. I try to emulate that crispy edge in the final minutes of this recipe by taking advantage of the pellet grill's high temperature setting. Yummy!

1. In a medium bowl, combine the lamb, salt, pepper, oregano, garlic, and onion powder; mix well. Cover with plastic wrap and refrigerate overnight.

2. Supply your smoker with wood pellets and follow the manufacturer's specific start-up procedure. Preheat, with the lid closed, to 300°F.

3. Remove the meat mixture from the refrigerator and, on a Frogmat or a piece of heavy-duty aluminum foil, roll and shape it into a rectangular loaf about 8 inches long by 5 inches wide.

4. Place the loaf directly on the grill, close the lid, and smoke for 35 minutes, or until a meat thermometer inserted in the center reads 155°F.

5. Remove the loaf from the heat and increase the temperature to 450°F.

6. Cut the loaf into ⅛-inch slices and place on a Frogmat or a piece of heavy-duty foil.

7. Return the meat (still on the Frogmat or foil) to the smoker, close the lid, and continue cooking for 2 to 4 minutes, or until the edges are crispy.

8. Warm the pitas in the smoker for a few minutes and serve with the lamb, tzatziki sauce, chopped tomato, and sliced onion.

Pair It **Serve the gyros with Sweet Potato Chips (page 152).**

VENISON STEAKS

Serves 4

PREP TIME: 10 MINUTES

SMOKE TIME: 1 HOUR 20 MINUTES

 SMOKE
TEMPERATURE:
225°F

 WOOD PELLETS:
HICKORY OR CHERRY

4 (8-ounce) venison steaks

2 tablespoons extra-virgin olive oil

4 garlic cloves, minced

1 tablespoon ground sage

2 teaspoons sea salt

2 teaspoons freshly ground black pepper

Game meat is almost always leaner than the meat of farm-raised hogs or cows that are usually bred for tenderness and fat marbling. So be aware that overcooking can really toughen venison. Online markets, such as Dartagnan.com, have sprung up with plenty of venison options, and you can likely also find sources from wild game meat processors used by local hunters.

1. Supply your smoker with wood pellets and follow the manufacturer's specific start-up procedure. Preheat, with the lid closed, to 225°F.

2. Rub the venison steaks well with the olive oil and season with the garlic, sage, salt, and pepper.

3. Arrange the venison steaks directly on the grill grate, close the lid, and smoke for 1 hour and 20 minutes, or until a meat thermometer inserted in the center reads 130°F to 140°F, depending on desired doneness. If you want a better sear, remove the steaks from the grill at an internal temperature of 125°F, crank up the heat to 450°F, or the "High" setting, and cook the steaks on each side for an additional 2 to 3 minutes.

Pair It   The earthy flavor of a venison steak, with its hints of acorn nuttiness, goes especially well with the sweetness of sweet potato. Pair these steaks with Sweet Potato Chips (page 152).

GREEK LEG OF LAMB

Serves 12 to 16

MARINATING TIME: 4 HOURS
PREP TIME: 15 MINUTES
SMOKE TIME: 20 TO 25 MINUTES
PER POUND

 SMOKE
TEMPERATURE:
325°F

 WOOD PELLETS:
OAK

2 tablespoons finely chopped
fresh rosemary

1 tablespoon ground thyme

5 garlic cloves, minced

2 tablespoons sea salt

1 tablespoon freshly ground
black pepper

Butcher's string

1 whole boneless (6- to
8-pound) leg of lamb

¼ cup extra-virgin olive oil

1 cup red wine vinegar

½ cup canola oil

Barbecue is regional across the United States. Even Kentucky has its foot in the ring. Leg of mutton is that foot. Long ago, Kentucky was the top lamb producer in the country, and that legacy lives on—mutton is still a traditional barbecue dish there, served with a savory black sauce. Over the years, mutton has lost out in popularity to lamb (which is the same animal, just under one year of age). The recipe here outlines the more traditional leg of lamb cooking method, but if you crave a variation, it can also be slow-smoked Kentucky mutton style (to a fall-apart internal temp of 205°F), like our Party Pulled Pork Shoulder (page 72).

1. In a small bowl, combine the rosemary, thyme, garlic, salt, and pepper; set aside.

2. Using butcher's string, tie the leg of lamb into the shape of a roast. Your butcher should also be happy to truss the leg for you.

3. Rub the lamb generously with the olive oil and season with the spice mixture. Transfer to a plate, cover with plastic wrap, and refrigerate for 4 hours.

4. Remove the lamb from the refrigerator but do not rinse.

5. Supply your smoker with wood pellets and follow the manufacturer's specific start-up procedure. Preheat, with the lid closed, to 325°F.

6. In a small bowl, combine the red wine vinegar and canola oil for basting.

7. Place the lamb directly on the grill, close the lid, and smoke for 20 to 25 minutes per pound (depending on desired doneness), basting with the oil and vinegar mixture every 30 minutes. Lamb is generally served medium-rare to medium, so it will be done when a meat thermometer inserted in the thickest part reads 140°F to 145°F.

8. Let the lamb rest for about 15 minutes before slicing to serve.

Pair It Try serving this lamb with Caprese Salad with Cold-Smoked Mozzarella (page 170).

Chapter 8
VEGETABLES AND SIDES

Man (and woman) cannot live on meat alone. Wood pellet grill owners can enjoy cooking and smoking high- or low-temperature veggies and tasty sides with ease. I like creating side dishes on the grill so much, I wrote my first cookbook about it (see Resources, page 196). Because most vegetables have shorter cook times than the meats you smoke, you can prep your veggie sides during the downtime and throw them on the grill in the last minutes of cooking—it's all conveniently coordinated!

The wood pellet grill's high-temperature settings allow for effortless baking and browning. Grilled vegetables offer you a far greater variety of flavors to discover than just meat, and the colors can be a dazzling feast for the eyes—especially in the summer months, when the farmers' market is bursting with fresh, locally grown fruit and vegetables. Finally, grilling outside is also the best way to keep your home cool in the hot summer months. ♦

◀ MEXICAN STREET CORN WITH CHIPOTLE BUTTER, page 149

CUTS

Veggies come in all shapes and sizes, and different dishes call for different cuts. Eggplant can be roasted whole to be blended into a delicious baba ghanouj, or sliced into thick disks and seasoned for a simple side. Onions can be sliced and grilled for more smoky surface area, or you can fight some tears, cut out the cores, stuff them with butter, and smoke them whole.

We shuck the corn on the cob in this book, but many people prefer to simply remove the silks and grill the whole corn with the husk intact. Root vegetables roast nicely with the higher temperatures of the wood pellet grill, but potatoes can take quite a long time to cook through. Cutting them in half first will greatly reduce cook time.

Vegetables may take a bit longer to prepare on wood pellet grills, but they actually absorb smoke much faster than meat.

TECHNIQUES

Just like meat, there are easy ways to make smoked vegetables and sides even better on the grill. First, marinating vegetables prior to smoking is a great way to tenderize them, as is cooking them in a moist environment. It is also a smart idea to cut similar vegetables into uniform sizes, shapes, and thicknesses to allow for even cook times.

RULES TO GRILL BY

When adding vegetables to your smoker, keep the following in mind for the yummiest results:

★ The water pan is your best friend. This will keep the moisture circulating in the smoking chamber.

★ Wash all of your produce thoroughly. Refer to the "Dirty Dozen" list (www.ewg.org) and consider buying organic. Such smoker favorites as peaches, peppers, and potatoes are on the list of most contaminated vegetables.

★ Marinades help add flavors to vegetables as much as they do to meat—and often more so. Eggplant and zucchini are like sponges for absorbing liquid marinades.

★ If you're cooking vegetables along with your main meat dish, consider their cook times and share the smoker space accordingly.

★ Most veggies don't require anything but a little salt, pepper, and smoke to taste great. But you'll also want to add a light brushing of olive oil to keep them from sticking to the grate, or use Frogmats.

★ Roasted veggies take on an a dense, almost magical texture on your wood pellet grill. 425°F is the sweet spot for roasting when you start with a fully preheated grill.

MEXICAN STREET CORN WITH CHIPOTLE BUTTER

Serves 4

PREP TIME: 10 MINUTES

SMOKE TIME: 12 TO 14 MINUTES

 SMOKE TEMPERATURE: 450°F

 WOOD PELLETS: HICKORY OR MESQUITE

4 ears corn

½ cup sour cream

½ cup mayonnaise

¼ cup chopped fresh cilantro, plus more for garnish

Chipotle Butter (page 185), for topping

1 cup grated Parmesan cheese

Corn on the cob has always made great barbecue food. You can cook it in the husk or out of the husk wrapped in foil, and it's nearly impossible to burn. Plus, it's handheld! The only trick has been getting the salt and butter to stick. We fix that by pouring on a spicy butter topping and wrapping the corn in foil to cook. It's finished with a topping of salty fresh Parmesan cheese, so every bite is coated with flavor and there's no fumbling around trying to butter your cob.

1. Supply your smoker with wood pellets and follow the manufacturer's specific start-up procedure. Preheat, with the lid closed, to 450°F.

2. Shuck the corn, removing the silks and cutting off the cores.

3. Tear four squares of aluminum foil large enough to completely cover an ear of corn.

4. In a medium bowl, combine the sour cream, mayonnaise, and cilantro. Slather the mixture all over the ears of corn.

5. Wrap each ear of corn in a piece of foil, sealing tightly. Place on the grill, close the lid, and smoke for 12 to 14 minutes.

6. Remove the corn from the foil and place in a shallow baking dish. Top with chipotle butter, the Parmesan cheese, and more chopped cilantro.

7. Serve immediately.

Smoking Tip After the initial 12- to 14-minute cook time, move the corn to indirect heat to keep warm as you cook the rest of your meal. It's very difficult to burn corn on the cob.

TWICE-SMOKED POTATOES

Serves 16

PREP TIME: 20 MINUTES

SMOKE TIME: 1 HOUR 35 MINUTES

 SMOKE
TEMPERATURE:
400°F, 375°F

 WOOD PELLETS:
MAPLE OR PECAN

8 Idaho, Russet, or Yukon Gold potatoes

1 (12-ounce) can evaporated milk, heated

1 cup (2 sticks) butter, melted

½ cup sour cream, at room temperature

1 cup grated Parmesan cheese

½ pound bacon, cooked and crumbled

¼ cup chopped scallions

Salt

Freshly ground black pepper

1 cup shredded Cheddar cheese

With twice the smoke and twice the flavor, these potatoes are the ideal side for steak or any smoked beef. They're so hearty they can almost hold their own as a main course. Shop for starchy baking potatoes with a thick skin, such as the traditional Russet or Idaho, and skip wrapping them in foil.

1. Supply your smoker with wood pellets and follow the manufacturer's specific start-up procedure. Preheat, with the lid closed, to 400°F.

2. Poke the potatoes all over with a fork. Arrange them directly on the grill grate, close the lid, and smoke for 1 hour and 15 minutes, or until cooked through and they have some give when pinched.

3. Let the potatoes cool for 10 minutes, then cut in half lengthwise.

4. Into a medium bowl, scoop out the potato flesh, leaving ¼ inch in the shells; place the shells on a baking sheet.

5. Using an electric mixer on medium speed, beat the potatoes, milk, butter, and sour cream until smooth.

6. Stir in the Parmesan cheese, bacon, and scallions, and season with salt and pepper.

7. Generously stuff each shell with the potato mixture and top with Cheddar cheese.

8. Place the baking sheet on the grill grate, close the lid, and smoke for 20 minutes, or until the cheese is melted.

Technique Tip One extra step can give your potato a salty crust. Before baking, cover the raw potato with your choice of oil, bacon grease (YAASS!), or butter, then coat the spud with sea salt.

ROASTED OKRA

Serves 3 to 4

PREP TIME: 10 MINUTES

SMOKE TIME: 30 MINUTES

 SMOKE
TEMPERATURE:
400°F

 WOOD PELLETS:
HICKORY OR
MESQUITE

Nonstick cooking spray or
butter, for greasing

1 pound whole okra

2 tablespoons extra-virgin
olive oil

2 teaspoons seasoned salt

2 teaspoons freshly ground
black pepper

As with many of the higher-temperature recipes in this book, this one can be prepared on the grill or in the oven if you need to conserve grill space. You may think of okra as a product of the American South, but its geographical origins trace back to South Asia, Ethiopia, and West Africa. From there it made its way to North and South America via the slave trade.

1. Supply your smoker with wood pellets and follow the manufacturer's specific start-up procedure. Preheat, with the lid closed, to 400°F. Alternatively, preheat your oven to 400°F.

2. Line a shallow rimmed baking pan with aluminum foil and coat with cooking spray.

3. Arrange the okra on the pan in a single layer. Drizzle with the olive oil, turning to coat. Season on all sides with the salt and pepper.

4. Place the baking pan on the grill grate, close the lid, and smoke for 30 minutes, or until crisp and slightly charred. Alternatively, roast in the oven for 30 minutes.

5. Serve hot.

Smoking Tip Whether you make this okra in the oven or in your wood pellet grill, be sure to fully preheat the oven or cook chamber for the best results.

SWEET POTATO CHIPS

Serves 2 to 3

SOAKING TIME: 15 TO 20 MINUTES
PREP TIME: 20 MINUTES
SMOKE TIME: 35 TO 45 MINUTES

 SMOKE
TEMPERATURE:
375°F

 WOOD PELLETS:
MAPLE

2 sweet potatoes

1 quart warm water

1 tablespoon cornstarch, plus
2 teaspoons

¼ cup extra-virgin olive oil

1 tablespoon salt

1 tablespoon packed
brown sugar

1 teaspoon ground cinnamon

1 teaspoon freshly ground
black pepper

½ teaspoon cayenne pepper

I am what I am, but it may not be a yam. All yams are sweet potatoes, but a yam is only one of many varieties of sweet potatoes. But all sweet potatoes enjoy the title of superfood. They are loaded with beta carotene, which is an antioxidant and provides vitamin A in abundance. Sweet potatoes are naturally sweet, but their natural sugars are slowly released into the bloodstream, ensuring a balanced source of energy without causing the blood sugar spikes that are linked to fatigue and weight gain. Sweet *and* healthy? Win-win!

1. Using a mandoline, thinly slice the sweet potatoes.

2. Pour the warm water into a large bowl and add 1 tablespoon of cornstarch and the potato slices. Let soak for 15 to 20 minutes.

3. Supply your smoker with wood pellets and follow the manufacturer's specific start-up procedure. Preheat, with the lid closed, to 375°F.

4. Drain the potato slices, then arrange in a single layer on a perforated pizza pan or a baking sheet lined with aluminum foil. Brush the potato slices on both sides with the olive oil.

5. In a small bowl, whisk together the salt, brown sugar, cinnamon, black pepper, cayenne pepper, and the remaining 2 teaspoons of cornstarch. Sprinkle this seasoning blend on both sides of the potatoes.

6. Place the pan or baking sheet on the grill grate, close the lid, and smoke for 35 to 45 minutes, flipping after 20 minutes, until the chips curl up and become crispy.

7. Store in an airtight container.

Ingredient Tip Avoid storing your sweet potatoes in the refrigerator's produce bin, which tends to give them a hard center and an unpleasant flavor. What, you don't have a root cellar? Just keep them in a cool, dry area of your kitchen.

BROCCOLI-CAULIFLOWER SALAD

Serves 6 to 8

PREP TIME: 25 MINUTES

1½ cups mayonnaise

½ cup sour cream

¼ cup sugar

1 bunch broccoli, cut into small pieces

1 head cauliflower, cut into small pieces

1 small red onion, chopped

6 slices bacon, cooked and crumbled (precooked bacon works well)

1 cup shredded Cheddar cheese

When I was a kid, I had a drug problem, meaning my parents "drug" me to church. These days, I enjoy church and have discovered some of the best recipes at potlucks, made by great church-member chefs. I am a slaw fanatic, and my favorite Southern Slaw (page 156) came directly from my church friend Fran Bendure. Recently, I discovered that Fran also has this recipe in her arsenal, and it almost seems like a sequel to that slaw. The flavors are quite similar.

1. In a small bowl, whisk together the mayonnaise, sour cream, and sugar to make a dressing.

2. In a large bowl, combine the broccoli, cauliflower, onion, bacon, and Cheddar cheese.

3. Pour the dressing over the vegetable mixture and toss well to coat.

4. Serve the salad chilled.

Ingredient Tip I like using precooked bacon for barbecue recipes. First of all, it saves a lot of time; second of all, *grilling* bacon is just a pain.

BUNNY DOGS WITH SWEET AND SPICY JALAPEÑO RELISH

Serves 8

PREP TIME: 20 MINUTES

SMOKE TIME: 35 TO 40 MINUTES

 SMOKE TEMPERATURE: 375°F

 WOOD PELLETS: CHERRY

8 hot dog-size carrots, peeled

¼ cup honey

¼ cup yellow mustard

Nonstick cooking spray or butter, for greasing

Salt

Freshly ground black pepper

8 hot dog buns

Sweet and Spicy Jalapeño Relish (page 192)

I first discovered these grilled carrots at Charleston's favorite area hot dog joint, Jack's Cosmic Dogs. I ordered the dish on a whim (I didn't realize I was going vegetarian), but loved it. Roast the carrots until they are golden brown, and be sure to enjoy with your favorite toppings.

1. Prepare the carrots by removing the stems and slicing in half lengthwise.

2. In a small bowl, whisk together the honey and mustard.

3. Supply your smoker with wood pellets and follow the manufacturer's specific start-up procedure. Preheat, with the lid closed, to 375°F.

4. Line a baking sheet with aluminum foil and coat with cooking spray.

5. Brush the carrots on both sides with the honey mustard and season with salt and pepper; put on the baking sheet.

6. Place the baking sheet on the grill grate, close the lid, and smoke for 35 to 40 minutes, or until tender and starting to brown.

7. To serve, lightly toast the hot dog buns on the grill and top each with two slices of carrot and some relish.

Smoking Tip Be sure to fully preheat your smoker to the temperature called for before placing carrots (or any roasting vegetables) on the grill.

BRUSSELS SPROUT BITES WITH CILANTRO-BALSAMIC DRIZZLE

Serves 4 to 6

PREP TIME: 15 MINUTES

SMOKE TIME: 45 MINUTES TO
1 HOUR

 SMOKE
TEMPERATURE:
300°F

 WOOD PELLETS:
MAPLE

16 to 20 long toothpicks

1 pound Brussels sprouts,
trimmed and wilted,
leaves removed

½ pound bacon, cut in half

1 tablespoon packed
brown sugar

1 tablespoon Cajun seasoning

¼ cup balsamic vinegar

¼ cup extra-virgin olive oil

¼ cup chopped fresh cilantro

2 teaspoons minced garlic

Brussels sprouts have become a popular appetizer and side dish in fine restaurants, but they're nothing new. In fact, they have been popular for ages in Brussels, Belgium, and I presume that's the origin of the name. There are myriad cooking options, from sautéing to pickling, but fire-roasting brings out some of the best flavors.

1. Soak the toothpicks in water for 15 minutes.

2. Supply your smoker with wood pellets and follow the manufacturer's specific start-up procedure. Preheat, with the lid closed, to 300°F.

3. Wrap each Brussels sprout in a half slice of bacon and secure with a toothpick.

4. In a small bowl, combine the brown sugar and Cajun seasoning. Dip each wrapped Brussels sprout in this sweet rub and roll around to coat.

5. Place the sprouts on a Frogmat or parchment paper–lined baking sheet on the grill grate, close the lid, and smoke for 45 minutes to 1 hour, turning as needed, until cooked evenly and the bacon is crisp.

6. In a small bowl, whisk together the balsamic vinegar, olive oil, cilantro, and garlic.

7. Remove the toothpicks from the Brussels sprouts, transfer to a plate and serve drizzled with the cilantro-balsamic sauce.

Ingredient Tip When fully cooked, Brussels sprouts often emit a sulfur-like smell—just another great reason to cook outdoors!

SOUTHERN SLAW

Serves 10 to 12

REFRIGERATING TIME: 1 HOUR
PREP TIME: 10 MINUTES

1 head cabbage, shredded

¼ cup white vinegar

¼ cup sugar

1 teaspoon paprika

½ teaspoon salt

½ teaspoon freshly ground black pepper

1 cup heavy (whipping) cream

I'm unapologetically weird. My favorite food of all time is slaw. I like all different styles, from tart to sweet, with carrots and even kale. But, as I mentioned in the recipe note for the Broccoli-Cauliflower Salad (page 153), *this* is the greatest coleslaw of all time.

1. Place the shredded cabbage in a large bowl.

2. In a small bowl, combine the vinegar, sugar, paprika, salt, and pepper.

3. Pour the vinegar mixture over the cabbage and mix well.

4. Fold in the heavy cream and refrigerate for at least 1 hour before serving.

Pair It Serve this slaw with Party Pulled Pork Shoulder (page 72), or with hot dogs and hamburgers, or with an hour of Netflix . . . Did I mention I *love* this slaw?

GEORGIA SWEET ONION BAKE

Serves 6 to 8

PREP TIME: 25 MINUTES

SMOKE TIME: 1 HOUR TO 1 HOUR
15 MINUTES

 SMOKE
TEMPERATURE:
350°F

 WOOD PELLETS:
MESQUITE

Nonstick cooking spray or
butter, for greasing

4 large Vidalia or other
sweet onions

8 tablespoons (1 stick) unsalted
butter, melted

4 chicken bouillon cubes

1 cup grated Parmesan cheese

This recipe relies on the perfect sweetness of a Vidalia onion. Vidalia is a city in Toombs County, Georgia, that was able to take full advantage of the low amount of sulfur in the soil there. The name Vidalia has been trademarked, and it's no surprise the Vidalia onion is Georgia's official state vegetable. Feel free to replace with other types of sweet onion, but if you can find Vidalia onions, get 'em!

1. Supply your smoker with wood pellets and follow the manufacturer's specific start-up procedure. Preheat, with the lid closed, to 350°F.

2. Coat a high-sided baking pan with cooking spray or butter.

3. Peel the onions and cut into quarters, separating into individual petals.

4. Spread the onions out in the prepared pan and pour the melted butter over them.

5. Crush the bouillon cubes and sprinkle over the buttery onion pieces, then top with the cheese.

6. Transfer the pan to the grill, close the lid, and smoke for 30 minutes.

7. Remove the pan from the grill, cover tightly with aluminum foil, and poke several holes all over to vent.

8. Place the pan back on the grill, close the lid, and smoke for an additional 30 to 45 minutes.

9. Uncover the onions, stir, and serve hot.

Ingredient Tip We use unsalted butter in many of the recipes in this book, mainly as a way to control the salt content of each dish.

CAROLINA BAKED BEANS

Serves 12 to 15

PREP TIME: 15 MINUTES

SMOKE TIME: 2 HOURS 30 MINUTES
TO 3 HOURS

 SMOKE
TEMPERATURE:
300°F

 WOOD PELLETS:
MESQUITE

3 (28-ounce) cans baked beans
(I like Bush's brand)

1 large onion, finely chopped

1 cup Bill's Best BBQ Sauce
(page 183)

½ cup light brown sugar

¼ cup Worcestershire sauce

3 tablespoons yellow mustard

Nonstick cooking spray or
butter, for greasing

1 large bell pepper, cut into
thin rings

½ pound thick-cut bacon,
partially cooked and cut into
quarters

Everyone touts Boston as the baked bean capital. Back in the day, the city was a big locale for distilling rum, and thus had an abundance of molasses. Bostonians added that surplus molasses to their bean recipes, and it was so good, the city earned the nickname "Beantown." In fact, baked beans and brown bread have been a traditional weekend meal in Massachusetts for generations. I've added some of my sweet barbecue sauce, mustard, bacon, onions, and bell pepper rings for a zesty Carolina twist.

1. Supply your smoker with wood pellets and follow the manufacturer's specific start-up procedure. Preheat, with the lid closed, to 300°F.

2. In a large mixing bowl, stir together the beans, onion, barbecue sauce, brown sugar, Worcestershire sauce, and mustard until well combined

3. Coat a 9-by-13-inch aluminum pan with cooking spray or butter.

4. Pour the beans into the pan and top with the bell pepper rings and bacon pieces, pressing them down slightly into the sauce.

5. Place a layer of heavy-duty foil on the grill grate to catch drips, and place the pan on top of the foil. Close the lid and cook for 2 hours 30 minutes to 3 hours, or until the beans are hot, thick, and bubbly.

6. Let the beans rest for 5 minutes before serving.

Smoking Tip You should usually avoid covering your grill grate with foil, but with these beans I recommend it, to protect from sticky spillover. A sheet or two under the shallow pan will do. Just keep the pan uncovered, to allow smoke to penetrate the surface of the beans.

BLT PASTA SALAD

Serves 10 to 12

PREP TIME: 20 MINUTES

SMOKE TIME: 30 TO 45 MINUTES

 SMOKE
TEMPERATURE:
225°F

 WOOD PELLETS:
HICKORY OR MAPLE

1 pound thick-cut bacon

16 ounces bowtie pasta,
cooked according to package
directions and drained

2 tomatoes, chopped

½ cup chopped scallions

½ cup Italian dressing

½ cup ranch dressing

1 tablespoon chopped
fresh basil

1 teaspoon salt

1 teaspoon freshly ground
black pepper

1 teaspoon garlic powder

1 head lettuce, cored and torn

If you don't like a classic BLT sandwich, stop right here! This cool summer pasta salad elevates the great flavors of the sandwich favorite. Hold the toast. Add pasta.

1. Supply your smoker with wood pellets and follow the manufacturer's specific start-up procedure. Preheat, with the lid closed, to 225°F.

2. Arrange the bacon slices on the grill grate, close the lid, and cook for 30 to 45 minutes, flipping after 20 minutes, until crisp.

3. Remove the bacon from the grill and chop.

4. In a large bowl, combine the chopped bacon with the cooked pasta, tomatoes, scallions, Italian dressing, ranch dressing, basil, salt, pepper, and garlic powder. Refrigerate until ready to serve.

5. Toss in the lettuce just before serving to keep it from wilting.

Ingredient Tip If you prefer a quicker method or a crispier outcome, smoke the bacon at 350°F for 6 to 7 minutes per side. Thick-cut bacon is easier to handle on the grill.

POTLUCK SALAD WITH SMOKED CORNBREAD

Serves 8 to 10

PREP TIME: 25 MINUTES

SMOKE TIME: 35 TO 45 MINUTES

 SMOKE
TEMPERATURE:
375°F

 WOOD PELLETS: OAK,
APPLE, OR PECAN

FOR THE CORNBREAD

1 cup all-purpose flour

1 cup yellow cornmeal

1 tablespoon sugar

2 teaspoons baking powder

1 teaspoon salt

1 cup milk

1 egg, beaten, at room
temperature

4 tablespoons (½ stick)
unsalted butter, melted
and cooled

Nonstick cooking spray or
butter, for greasing

Sure, you can make the cornbread for this recipe in your kitchen oven, but I suggest breaking out a cast iron skillet and taking advantage of the baking capabilities of your wood pellet grill. If ya got it, why not flaunt it? But even if you decide to bake a box of Jiffy cornbread mix, I urge you to try it just once on the smoker.

TO MAKE THE CORNBREAD

1. In a medium bowl, combine the flour, cornmeal, sugar, baking powder, and salt.

2. In a small bowl, whisk together the milk and egg. Pour in the butter, then slowly fold this mixture into the dry ingredients.

3. Supply your smoker with wood pellets and follow the manufacturer's specific start-up procedure. Preheat, with the lid closed, to 375°F.

4. Coat a cast iron skillet with cooking spray or butter.

5. Pour the batter into the skillet, place on the grill grate, close the lid, and smoke for 35 to 45 minutes, or until the cornbread is browned and pulls away from the side of the skillet.

6. Remove the cornbread from the grill and let cool, then coarsely crumble.

FOR THE SALAD

½ cup milk

½ cup sour cream

2 tablespoons dry ranch
dressing mix

1 pound bacon, cooked and
crumbled

3 tomatoes, chopped

1 bell pepper, chopped

1 cucumber, seeded
and chopped

2 stalks celery, chopped
(about 1 cup)

½ cup chopped scallions

TO MAKE THE SALAD

1. In a small bowl, whisk together the milk, sour cream, and ranch
   dressing mix.

2. In a medium bowl, combine the crumbled bacon, tomatoes, bell
   pepper, cucumber, celery, and scallions.

3. In a large serving bowl, layer half of the crumbled cornbread, half
   of the bacon-veggie mixture, and half of the dressing. Toss lightly.

4. Repeat the layering with the remaining cornbread, bacon-veggie
   mixture, and dressing. Toss again.

5. Refrigerate the salad for at least 1 hour. Serve cold.

Smoking Tip As shown throughout this book, cast iron skillet
can be a great partner for your wood pellet grill. It can be used to
brown steaks as easily as it can be used as a baking pan. Plus, cast
iron retains heat well after you take it to the table for serving.

WATERMELON-BERRY BOWL

Serves 4 to 6

PREP TIME: 10 MINUTES

1 pint strawberries, hulled and cut in half

1 pint blackberries

1 pint blueberries

1 pint raspberries

1 (20-ounce) can pineapple chunks, drained

4 cups watermelon cubes (1 inch)

Juice of 1 lemon

¼ cup sugar

Nothing says summertime like a chilled fruit salad with plenty of watermelon. If you're feeling creative, you can serve it in the hollowed-out watermelon shell. Extra points if you carve the watermelon rind to include a basket handle.

1. In a large bowl, combine the strawberries, blackberries, blueberries, raspberries, pineapple chunks, and watermelon cubes.

2. Stir in the lemon juice and sugar.

3. Refrigerate for at least 1 hour before serving.

Serving Tip Keep your fruit salad cold at all times. I recommend placing a pan filled with ice underneath it to keep your serving bowl chilled, especially if you're enjoying your meal outside.

BACON-WRAPPED JALAPEÑO POPPERS

Serves 10 to 12

PREP TIME: 20 MINUTES

SMOKE TIME: 30 MINUTES

 SMOKE
TEMPERATURE:
350°F

 WOOD PELLETS:
MAPLE OR HICKORY

8 ounces cream cheese, softened

½ cup shredded Cheddar cheese

¼ cup chopped scallions

1 teaspoon chipotle chile powder or regular chili powder

1 teaspoon garlic powder

1 teaspoon salt

18 large jalapeño peppers, stemmed, seeded, and halved lengthwise

1 pound bacon (precooked works well)

These poppers differ from Scotch Eggs (page 73) and armadillo eggs because the peppers are stuffed and wrapped in bacon instead of sausage. This recipe also works with the "pepper rack" vertical pepper holder you may have seen marketed for grilling. Just stuff them from the top down.

1. Supply your smoker with wood pellets and follow the manufacturer's specific start-up procedure. Preheat, with the lid closed, to 350°F. Line a baking sheet with aluminum foil.

2. In a small bowl, combine the cream cheese, Cheddar cheese, scallions, chipotle powder, garlic powder, and salt.

3. Stuff the jalapeño halves with the cheese mixture.

4. Cut the bacon into pieces big enough to wrap around the stuffed pepper halves.

5. Wrap the bacon around the peppers and place on the prepared baking sheet.

6. Put the baking sheet on the grill grate, close the lid, and smoke the peppers for 30 minutes, or until the cheese is melted and the bacon is cooked through and crisp.

7. Let the jalapeño poppers cool for 3 to 5 minutes. Serve warm.

Ingredient Tip Grilling bacon is made easier with the indirect heat of a wood pellet grill, but I still like to use precooked bacon to wrap these poppers. The peppers will fully cook as the bacon gets crisp and fully rendered.

SCAMPI SPAGHETTI SQUASH

Serves 4

PREP TIME: 20 MINUTES
SMOKE TIME: 40 MINUTES

 SMOKE
TEMPERATURE:
375°F

 WOOD PELLETS:
HICKORY

FOR THE SQUASH

1 spaghetti squash

2 tablespoons extra-virgin olive oil

1 teaspoon salt

1 teaspoon freshly ground black pepper

2 teaspoons garlic powder

The spaghetti squash has become my family's go-to pasta replacement. The stringy texture from which it gets its name allows you to replace noodles with a delicious low-carb substitute. The long cook time also allows the squash to absorb some nice smoky flavor. We've loved this rich scampi recipe at our house lately, but feel free to use the squash as a blank canvas for your favorite pasta sauce.

TO MAKE THE SQUASH

1. Supply your smoker with wood pellets and follow the manufacturer's specific start-up procedure. Preheat, with the lid closed, to 375°F.

2. Cut off both ends of the squash, then cut it in half lengthwise. Scoop out and discard the seeds.

3. Rub the squash flesh well with the olive oil and sprinkle on the salt, pepper, and garlic powder.

4. Place the squash cut-side up on the grill grate, close the lid, and smoke for 40 minutes, or until tender.

FOR THE SAUCE

4 tablespoons (½ stick) unsalted butter

½ cup white wine

1 tablespoon minced garlic

2 teaspoons chopped fresh parsley

1 teaspoon red pepper flakes

½ teaspoon salt

½ teaspoon freshly ground black pepper

TO MAKE THE SAUCE AND ASSEMBLE

1. On the stovetop, in a medium saucepan over medium heat, combine the butter, white wine, minced garlic, parsley, red pepper flakes, salt, and pepper, and cook for about 5 minutes, or until heated through. Reduce the heat to low and keep the sauce warm.

2. Remove the squash from the grill and let cool slightly before shredding the flesh with a fork; discard the skin.

3. Stir the shredded squash into the garlic-wine butter sauce and serve immediately.

Ingredient Tip Firm squash can be very tough to split without a razor-sharp knife. You can microwave the whole squash for 3 minutes to soften it just enough to make it easier to cut through.

Chapter 9

CHEESE, NUTS, BREADS, AND DESSERTS

T he magic of a wood pellet grill is that it's made to be controlled like your kitchen's oven while also harnessing the energy of hardwood combustion. It's great for maintaining low-and-slow temperatures as well as for baking at 350°F with ease. Some foods, like cheese and nuts, are perfect partners for smoke and salt. Breads and desserts are now a joy to make on the grill, and they also take on a smoky flavor. My wife, MJ, was amazed to learn we could experiment with cookies and pie on the wood pellet grill. She has since become much more involved with cooking on it. Thanks to the easy control of the kitchen oven-like thermostat, the sky is the limit with desserts on the grill. One added bonus during the summer months is that you can bake without heating up the kitchen. Plus, no added preservatives are needed because there won't be a scrap left over. . . . ◐

◀ SMOKED BLACKBERRY PIE, page 173

TECHNIQUES

Baking breads and smoking cheeses require different tactics. Baking is easy on the wood pellet grill, but smoking items like cheese can be a little trickier. To smoke cheese correctly, you need to employ a technique called "cold-smoking." You want only the smoke and not the heat from the fire pot inside your smoker. Many wood pellet grills will need a cold-smoker attachment (sold separately) to sustain sub-100°F temperatures. Another option is the A-Maze-N smoker tubes that bypass the firebox all together.

RULES TO GRILL BY

For best results, keep the following tips in mind when venturing into breads, smoked-cheese dishes, and nuts:

★ Match your dessert or baked item with a lighter smoke from fruitwood. Or, if you are smoking pecans, use pecan wood pellets; match baked apples with applewood.

★ Breads will burn very quickly on any grill. Keep a close watch.

★ Be cool. Cold-smoking allows you to add smoky flavor without melting, cooking, or degrading the structure of a cheese. Most wood pellet smokers require a cold-smoking kit. Traeger and Rec Tec offer cold-smoke units that are sold separately. There are plenty of hacks on YouTube using dryer vent tubes that run from the smokestack to homemade cold boxes. However, in general, cold-smoking is not easy to do on most pellet grills.

★ No sweat. Start with room-temperature cheese, as chilled cheese may sweat. Blot and dry the cheese while it adjusts to room temperature. This will help it develop a better skin.

★ Let it rest. Just like meat, cheese needs to pause after smoking. A rest of at least 24 hours or up to 1 week in the refrigerator lets the flavors mellow and improve.

SWEET CHEESE MUFFINS

Makes 3 dozen mini muffins

PREP TIME: 15 MINUTES

SMOKE TIME: 12 TO 15 MINUTES

 SMOKE
TEMPERATURE:
375°F

 WOOD PELLETS:
MAPLE OR CHERRY

1 package butter cake mix

1 package Jiffy Corn Muffin Mix

1 cup self-rising or cake flour

12 tablespoons (1½ sticks) unsalted butter, softened, plus 8 tablespoons (1 stick) melted

3½ cups shredded Cheddar cheese

2 eggs, beaten, at room temperature

2¼ cups buttermilk

Nonstick cooking spray or butter, for greasing

¼ cup packed brown sugar

These muffins are a crowd-pleaser. But it's hard to stop at eating just one, so be careful when you serve them before the main course. Because your wood pellet grill can hold a steady baking temperature, you can use it to prepare these on the grill, but they are just as easy to make in your kitchen oven. They fall somewhere between a sweet muffin and savory cornbread. The secret ingredient is the cake mix. You won't have any of these muffins left over, I guarantee.

1. Supply your smoker with wood pellets and follow the manufacturer's specific start-up procedure. Preheat, with the lid closed, to 375°F.

2. In a large mixing bowl, combine the cake mix, corn muffin mix, and flour.

3. Slice the 1½ sticks of softened butter into pieces and cut into the dry ingredients. Add the cheese and mix thoroughly.

4. In a medium bowl, combine the eggs and buttermilk, then add to the dry ingredients, stirring until well blended.

5. Coat three 12-cup mini muffin pans with cooking spray and spoon ¼ cup of batter into each cup.

6. Transfer the pans to the grill, close the lid, and smoke, monitoring closely, for 12 to 15 minutes, or until the muffins are lightly browned.

7. While the muffins are cooking, make the topping: In a small bowl, stir together the remaining 1 stick of melted butter and the brown sugar until well combined.

8. Remove the muffins from the grill. Brush the tops with the sweet butter and serve warm.

Pair It These sweet muffins complement the tart meatiness of Baby Back Ribs (page 64).

CAPRESE SALAD WITH COLD-SMOKED MOZZARELLA

Serves 8 (makes 1 pound of cheese)

CHEESE MELLOWING
TIME: 1 TO 7 DAYS

PREP TIME: 10 MINUTES

SMOKE TIME: 2 HOURS

 SMOKE
TEMPERATURE:
80°F TO 90°F

 WOOD PELLETS:
APPLE

1 (1-pound) block fresh
mozzarella cheese, at room
temperature

4 large tomatoes

1 bunch fresh basil leaves

3 tablespoons extra-virgin
olive oil

2 tablespoons balsamic vinegar

1 teaspoon garlic powder

Salt

Freshly ground black pepper

Crusty French bread,
for serving

Cold-smoking cheese will require either a smoker tube like the A-Maze-N brand, or an accessory like a cold-smoking attachment. The process uses only smoke—no heat. Giving the mozzarella some time to mellow in the refrigerator will allow the smoke flavor to develop into the perfect enhancement for this caprese salad. For a visual touch, we prepare this Hasselback potato–style (see step 8).

1. Supply your smoker with wood pellets but do not follow the start-up procedure or preheat the smoker.

2. Cut the mozzarella into 4-by-2-inch blocks and blot completely dry before placing in the coolest area of the smoker.

3. With the smoker power off, ignite a full smoker tube on the grill grate to generate a long, slow source of smoke.

4. Keep the smoker below 90°F, using a pan of ice to lower the temperature if necessary.

5. Cold-smoke the cheese for 2 hours. When done, remove from the smoker and blot dry if needed.

6. Wrap the smoked cheese in wax or parchment paper and let it mellow in the refrigerator for at least 24 hours or up to 7 days.

7. Once mellowed, slice the cheese and set it aside.

8. Place 4 large tomatoes on a serving platter and slice each one Hasselback-style; that is, make 5 or 6 deep slices in each tomato without cutting all the way through, like a Hasselback potato.

9. Stuff the sliced smoked mozzarella and some of the basil leaves into the grooves of the tomatoes, then sprinkle the remaining basil leaves over everything.

10. Drizzle the tomatoes with the olive oil and balsamic vinegar. Top with garlic powder, season with salt and pepper, and serve with crusty French bread.

Ingredient Tip Try the same cold-smoking process for Cheddar, Gouda, Swiss, provolone, or pepper jack cheeses.

BACON CHOCOLATE CHIP COOKIES

Makes 2 dozen cookies

PREP TIME: 20 MINUTES

SMOKE TIME: 10 TO 12 MINUTES

 SMOKE
TEMPERATURE:
375°F

 WOOD PELLETS:
MAPLE

2¾ cups all-purpose flour

1½ teaspoons baking soda

½ teaspoon salt

12 tablespoons (1½ sticks)
unsalted butter, softened

1 cup light brown sugar

1 cup granulated sugar

2 eggs, at room temperature

2½ teaspoons apple
cider vinegar

1 teaspoon vanilla extract

2 cups semisweet
chocolate chips

8 slices bacon, cooked and
crumbled

Bacon salt, bacon lip balm, bacon whiskey . . . I've always
said bacon is the duct tape of food, but lately it's become an
obsession. So much so that there is an annual Baconfest in
Lathrop, California. The event features pig races, cooking
competitions, and the dreaded bacon eating contest. Sounds
gut-wrenching! These cookies bake just fine in the oven, but the
lick of smoke they get from hardwood fire makes them unique.
With or without the smoke, though, it seems everything's better
with bacon.

1. In a large bowl, combine the flour, baking soda, and salt, and mix well.

2. In a separate large bowl, using an electric mixer on medium speed,
cream the butter and sugars. Reduce the speed to low and mix in the
eggs, vinegar, and vanilla.

3. With the mixer speed still on low, slowly incorporate the dry ingredients, chocolate chips, and bacon pieces.

4. Supply your smoker with wood pellets and follow the manufacturer's
specific start-up procedure. Preheat, with the lid closed, to 375°F.

5. Line a large baking sheet with parchment paper.

6. Drop rounded teaspoonfuls of cookie batter onto the prepared baking
sheet and place on the grill grate. Close the lid and smoke for 10 to
12 minutes, or until the cookies are browned around the edges.

Smoking Tip Try to match your pellet hardwood to your bacon.
If you are using hickory-smoked bacon, use hickory pellets.

S'MORES DIP SKILLET

Serves 6 to 8

PREP TIME: 5 MINUTES

SMOKE TIME: 6 TO 8 MINUTES

 SMOKE
TEMPERATURE:
450°F

 WOOD PELLETS:
APPLE OR CHERRY

2 tablespoons salted
butter, melted

¼ cup milk

12 ounces semisweet
chocolate chips

16 ounces Jet-Puffed
marshmallows

Graham crackers and apple
wedges, for serving

It's always great to reflect on childhood memories when grilling. No recipe does that better than the Scout's classic, s'mores. My wife, MJ, perfected the treat for the grill and nailed the golden-brown marshmallow topping. This dip will leave *everyone* wanting s'more.

1. Supply your smoker with wood pellets and follow the manufacturer's specific start-up procedure. Preheat, with the lid closed, to 450°F.

2. Place a cast iron skillet on the preheated grill grate and pour in the melted butter and milk, stirring for about 1 minute.

3. Once the mixture starts to heat, top with the chocolate chips in an even layer and arrange the marshmallows standing up to cover all of the chocolate.

4. Close the lid and smoke for 5 to 7 minutes, or until the marshmallows are lightly toasted.

5. Remove from the heat and serve immediately with graham crackers and apple wedges for dipping.

Smoking Tip Your pellet grill will toast marshmallows easier than a raging campfire, but beware! Like bread, marshmallows will burn quickly on the grill, so keep a very close eye on them. And remember: no double dipping!

SMOKED BLACKBERRY PIE

Serves 8

PREP TIME: 15 MINUTES

SMOKE TIME: 20 TO 25 MINUTES

 SMOKE TEMPERATURE: 375°F

 WOOD PELLETS: APPLE OR CHERRY

Nonstick cooking spray or butter, for greasing

1 box (2 sheets) refrigerated piecrusts

8 tablespoons (1 stick) unsalted butter, melted, plus 8 tablespoons (1 stick) cut into pieces

½ cup all-purpose flour

2 cups sugar, divided

2 pints blackberries

½ cup milk

Vanilla ice cream, for serving

If you've ever picked wild blackberries, you may remember that they are actually red before they ripen. You may have heard the old expression, "Blackberries are red when they're green." In this recipe, the dark, plump blackberries are a feast for the eyes, and they're healthy, thanks to their high levels of dietary fiber, vitamin C, and vitamin K. I will therefore always have a second helping of this pie.

1. Supply your smoker with wood pellets and follow the manufacturer's specific start-up procedure. Preheat, with the lid closed, to 375°F.

2. Coat a cast iron skillet with cooking spray.

3. Unroll 1 refrigerated piecrust and place in the bottom and up the side of the skillet. Using a fork, poke holes in the crust in several places.

4. Set the skillet on the grill grate, close the lid, and smoke for 5 minutes, or until lightly browned. Remove from the grill and set aside.

5. In a large bowl, combine the stick of melted butter with the flour and 1½ cups of sugar.

6. Add the blackberries to the flour-sugar mixture and toss until well coated.

7. Spread the berry mixture evenly in the skillet and sprinkle the milk on top. Scatter half of the cut pieces of butter randomly over the mixture.

8. Unroll the remaining piecrust and place it over the top of skillet or slice the dough into even strips and weave it into a lattice. Scatter the remaining pieces of butter along the top of the crust.

9. Sprinkle the remaining ½ cup of sugar on top of the crust and return the skillet to the smoker.

10. Close the lid and smoke for 15 to 20 minutes, or until bubbly and brown on top. It may be necessary to use some aluminum foil around the edges near the end of the cooking time to prevent the crust from burning.

11. Serve the pie hot with vanilla ice cream.

Ingredient Tip If you opt to use different kinds of berries, remember that raspberries are delicate. Avoid washing them under hard running water; instead, place in a colander and immerse in a water bath.

CARROT CAKE ON THE BARBIE

Serves 12 to 16

PREP TIME: 20 MINUTES

SMOKE TIME: 1 HOUR

 SMOKE
TEMPERATURE:
350°F

 WOOD PELLETS:
APPLE OR CHERRY

FOR THE CAKE

8 carrots, peeled and grated

4 eggs, at room temperature

1 cup vegetable oil

½ cup milk

1 teaspoon vanilla extract

2 cups sugar

2 cups self-rising or cake flour

2 teaspoons baking soda

1 teaspoon salt

1 cup finely chopped pecans

Nonstick cooking spray or
butter, for greasing

No one really knows who came up with the idea of putting carrots in a cake, but it does have attributes that trace back to medieval times, when people would often make a carrot pudding. I guess the carrots add moisture and were something sweet when you couldn't find corn syrup. In fact, this carrot cake is the only vegetable cake I know of (I'm not counting zucchini bread as cake). It claims two spots in my food pyramid.

TO MAKE THE CAKE

1. Supply your smoker with wood pellets and follow the manufacturer's specific start-up procedure. Preheat, with the lid closed, to 350°F.

2. In a food processor or blender, combine the grated carrots, eggs, oil, milk, and vanilla, and process until the carrots are finely minced.

3. In a large mixing bowl, combine the sugar, flour, baking soda, and salt.

4. Add the carrot mixture to the flour mixture and stir until well incorporated. Fold in the chopped pecans.

5. Coat a 9-by-13-inch baking pan with cooking spray.

6. Pour the batter into prepared pan and place on the grill grate. Close the lid and smoke for about 1 hour, or until a toothpick inserted in the center comes out clean.

7. Remove the cake from the grill and let cool completely.

FOR THE FROSTING

8 ounces cream cheese

1 cup confectioners' sugar

8 tablespoons (1 stick) unsalted butter, at room temperature

1 teaspoon vanilla extract

½ teaspoon salt

2 tablespoons to ¼ cup milk

TO MAKE THE FROSTING

1. Using an electric mixer on low speed, beat the cream cheese, confectioners' sugar, butter, vanilla, and salt, adding 2 tablespoons to ¼ cup of milk to thin the frosting as needed.

2. Frost the cooled cake and slice to serve.

Ingredient Tip The carrot is the special ingredient here, and you want to avoid any large chunks. Use a handheld grater and be sure to protect your fingers by grasping the carrot with a kitchen towel.

BISCUIT AND GRAVY BREAKFAST BAKE

Serves 8 to 10

PREP TIME: 40 MINUTES

SMOKE TIME: 45 MINUTES

 SMOKE TEMPERATURE: 350°F

 WOOD PELLETS: HICKORY

8 tablespoons (1 stick) unsalted butter

½ cup all-purpose flour

6½ cups milk, divided

1 onion, chopped

2 tablespoons minced garlic

1 tablespoon Worcestershire sauce

2 teaspoons hot sauce

2 teaspoons red pepper flakes

2 teaspoons salt

2 teaspoons freshly ground black pepper

2 pounds ground sausage, cooked and crumbled

1 (20-ounce) package shredded hash brown potatoes

20 refrigerated or thawed frozen biscuits

2 cups shredded sharp Cheddar cheese

10 eggs, beaten

Nonstick cooking spray or butter, for greasing

This hearty baked breakfast dish is a nice way to feed a group on a summer morning without heating up the kitchen. Close your eyes and let the smoke help you imagine that you're cooking on an antique wood stove.

1. On the stovetop, in a skillet over medium heat, melt the butter.

2. Whisk in the flour, stirring constantly for 1 minute.

3. Gradually add 6 cups of milk, the onion, garlic, Worcestershire sauce, hot sauce, red pepper flakes, salt, and pepper.

4. Continue cooking for 2 minutes, then fold in the cooked sausage; set the mixture aside.

5. Supply your smoker with wood pellets and follow the manufacturer's specific start-up procedure. Preheat, with the lid closed, to 350°F.

6. Line a 9-by-13-inch baking pan with aluminum foil and coat with cooking spray.

7. Spread the hash browns in the bottom of the pan and top with the biscuits. Cover with the shredded cheese.

8. In a medium bowl, combine the beaten eggs and remaining ½ cup of milk. Pour this mixture over the cheese in the pan, then top with the sausage gravy.

9. Place the pan on the grill grate, close the lid, and smoke for 45 minutes, or until bubbly.

10. Serve the breakfast bake hot.

Smoker Tip   Speaking of biscuits . . . I like to use refrigerated or frozen (unthawed) biscuits to help me learn about any hot spots on the grill. Preheat your grill to 350°F , then spread the 20 or so biscuits evenly across the grate. Flip after 5 minutes and make note (take a cell phone photo) of any uneven browning.

ICE CREAM BREAD

Serves 12 to 16

PREP TIME: 10 MINUTES

SMOKE TIME: 50 MINUTES TO 1 HOUR

 SMOKE TEMPERATURE: 350°F

 WOOD PELLETS: APPLE OR CHERRY

1 (1½-quart) tub full-fat butter pecan ice cream, well softened (but not melted)

4 cups self-rising or cake flour

1 cup sugar

1 teaspoon salt

2 cups semisweet chocolate chips

Nonstick cooking spray or butter, for greasing

8 tablespoons (1 stick) butter, melted

Like me, you have probably seen the unbelievable claims of two-ingredient ice cream bread on the Internet. Does it live up to the hype? No! But I added three basic ingredients, and it was amazing. It's not a cake; it's a delicious, lightly sweetened breakfast or snack bread, similar to banana bread. Whatever you do, don't use fat-free ice cream—the bread needs the fat for moisture.

1. Supply your smoker with wood pellets and follow the manufacturer's specific start-up procedure. Preheat, with the lid closed, to 350°F.

2. In a large bowl, combine the softened ice cream, flour, sugar, and salt, and beat with an electric mixer on medium speed for 2 minutes.

3. With the mixer still on medium speed, add the chocolate chips and beat until well blended.

4. Coat an angel food cake tube pan or Bundt cake pan with cooking spray. (Note: I tried this in a cast iron Dutch oven, but it took too long to cook—the center was still mushy and the outside too dry. It needs the benefit of the tube in the middle to cook evenly in a shorter amount of time.)

5. Pour the batter into the prepared pan and level out the top.

6. Place the cake pan in the center of the grill, close the lid, and smoke for 50 minutes to 1 hour, or until a toothpick inserted in the center comes out clean.

7. Remove the pan from the grill and let the bread cool for 10 minutes before removing from the pan and slicing. Serve drizzled with the melted butter.

Substitution Tip Try cookies and cream or any other flavor of ice cream, or stir in 5 mashed ripe bananas or 1 cup peanut butter—it's your canvas.

SPICY BBQ PECANS

Makes 2 cups

PREP TIME: 10 MINUTES

SMOKE TIME: 1 HOUR

 SMOKE
TEMPERATURE:
225°F

 WOOD PELLETS:
HICKORY OR
MESQUITE

Nonstick cooking spray or
butter, for greasing

3 tablespoons unsalted
butter, melted

2½ teaspoons garlic powder

2 teaspoons salt

1 teaspoon freshly ground
black pepper

1 teaspoon onion powder

1 teaspoon dried thyme

2 cups (16 ounces) raw
pecan halves

Pecans are a classic South Carolina nut. You can make it easy for the smoke to adhere to them by starting with a wet coating and grill pan (or a tray with plenty of holes). Frogmats are heat-resistant, nonstick mesh mats that are perfect for letting smoke flow around your food. They're also machine-washable. You can add even more spice to your pecans with cayenne, cumin, chili powder, nutmeg, or cocoa powder.

1. Supply your smoker with wood pellets and follow the manufacturer's specific start-up procedure. Preheat, with the lid closed, to 225°F.

2. Line a rimmed baking sheet with parchment paper or aluminum foil and coat with cooking spray.

3. In a large bowl, stir together the butter, garlic powder, salt, pepper, onion powder, and dried thyme. Add the pecans and stir until well coated.

4. Arrange the nuts in a single layer on the prepared baking sheet and place on the grill grate.

5. Close the lid and smoke for about 1 hour, turning once, until heated through and toasted.

6. Remove from the grill to let cool and dry.

7. Store in an airtight container for up to 3 weeks.

Ingredient Tip Nuts are widely available already roasted, but you need raw nuts for this recipe. You can find the freshest selection at Whole Foods and Trader Joe's.

QUATTRO FORMAGGI MACARONI AND CHEESE

Serves 8

PREP TIME: 25 MINUTES
SMOKE TIME: 1 HOUR

 SMOKE
TEMPERATURE:
225°F

 WOOD PELLETS:
HICKORY OR
MESQUITE

4 tablespoons (½ stick)
unsalted butter

¼ cup all-purpose flour

3 cups milk

3 teaspoons garlic powder

2 teaspoons salt

1 teaspoon freshly ground
black pepper

2 cups shredded Cheddar
cheese, divided

2 cups shredded Monterey
Jack cheese

1 cup grated Parmesan cheese

8 ounces cream cheese, cut
into cubes

1 pound elbow macaroni
noodles, cooked according
to package directions

Nonstick cooking spray or
butter, for greasing

Four cheeses in a recipe that serves eight equals one happy camper. You'll be too sleepy to do the math after indulging in this smoked comfort food.

1. On the stovetop, in a large saucepan over medium heat, melt the butter. Whisk in the flour, stirring constantly for 1 minute. Stir in the milk, garlic powder, salt, and pepper, and bring to a boil.

2. Reduce the heat to low and cook for 5 minutes, or until thickened. Remove from the heat.

3. Add 1½ cups of Cheddar, the Monterey Jack, Parmesan, and cream cheese, and stir until melted. Fold in the cooked pasta.

4. Supply your smoker with wood pellets and follow the manufacturer's specific start-up procedure. Preheat, with the lid closed, to 225°F.

5. Coat a 9-by-13-inch baking pan with cooking spray.

6. Pour the macaroni and cheese into the pan and place on the grill to absorb some delicious wood smoke. Close the lid and smoke for 1 hour, or until bubbly. Top with the remaining ½ cup of Cheddar cheese during the last 20 minutes of cooking.

7. Serve the macaroni and cheese hot.

Pair It **Double your paper plate and enjoy with Baby Back Ribs (page 64).**

Chapter 10

RUBS, SAUCES, AND MORE

My first thought when I visit a new barbecue restaurant is "Do I smell smoke?" If you are really smoking meat to perfection, the sauce is secondary to the smoke. In fact, some really proud pit masters scoff at saucing the meat and ask that it only be served on the side. I also think sauce is great on the side and best used sparingly during the cook. I recommend using a rub *before* smoking, and using a sauce at the *end*, more as a glaze.

A good sauce allows you to regionalize your dish. South Carolina has mustard-based sauces. I give away a great recipe in my free book, *Sides & Sauces*, on my website (see Resources on page 196). North Carolina uses vinegar-based sauces; Alabama has an unusual white sauce for chicken; and, of course, there's Kansas City's sweet, smoky sauce that is on store shelves nationwide as KC Masterpiece. ◊

◀ SWEET AND SPICY JALAPEÑO RELISH, page 192

SAUCE SUCCESS

Get sauced with these tips:

★ It may be tempting, but you should never reuse a marinade or sauce that has been basted on uncooked meat. It can spread foodborne illness. Instead, it is a good idea to reserve a portion of sauce at the beginning of the cook to enjoy later.

★ Freshly made sauces can keep safely for many days in the refrigerator, but if the sauce has been outside or out of refrigeration for longer than two hours, it should be discarded.

★ Sweet sauces can be quick to burn on the grill. Be sure to add them only during the final minutes of the cook.

★ Use nonreactive containers to prepare your sauces. Good choices are stainless steel, glass, enamel, and porcelain vessels that will not cause a chemical reaction when in contact with acidic foods.

★ If you want a thicker glaze of flavor on your barbecued meat, you can brush on layers of sauce repeatedly over the last 10 minutes of cooking, letting each layer firm up before adding another.

BILL'S BEST BBQ SAUCE

Makes 3 cups

PREP TIME: 10 MINUTES
COOK TIME: 30 MINUTES

1 small onion, finely chopped

2 garlic cloves, finely minced

2 cups ketchup

1 cup water

½ cup molasses

½ cup apple cider vinegar

5 tablespoons granulated sugar

5 tablespoons light
brown sugar

1 tablespoon
Worcestershire sauce

1 tablespoon freshly squeezed
lemon juice

2 teaspoons liquid smoke

1½ teaspoons freshly ground
black pepper

1 tablespoon yellow mustard

There's just something about the tangy zip of this sauce that keeps me going back to it time and time again. It's important to use freshly ground black pepper and a good-quality Worcestershire sauce that features anchovies. This sauce is good on everything from wings to ribs—and napkins, too. You read that right: It's so delicious, I might lick it off my napkin.

1. On the stovetop, in a saucepan over medium heat, combine the onion, garlic, ketchup, water, molasses, apple cider vinegar, granulated sugar, brown sugar, Worcestershire sauce, lemon juice, liquid smoke, pepper, and mustard. Bring to a boil, then reduce the heat to low and simmer for 30 minutes, straining out any bigger chunks, if desired.

2. Let the sauce cool completely, then transfer to an airtight container and refrigerate for up to 2 weeks, or use the canning process to store for longer.

Pair It   This sauce offers the perfect blend of sweet, tart, and smoky. Try it with barbecued chicken, in baked beans, with pulled pork or brisket, on pork tacos. . . .

CHIMICHURRI SAUCE

Makes 2 cups

PREP TIME: 5 MINUTES

½ cup extra-virgin olive oil

1 bunch fresh parsley, stems removed

1 bunch fresh cilantro, stems removed

1 small red onion, chopped

3 tablespoons dried oregano

1 tablespoon minced garlic

Juice of 1 lemon

2 tablespoons red wine vinegar

1 teaspoon salt

1 teaspoon freshly ground black pepper

1 teaspoon cayenne pepper

I love the freshness of chimichurri. Sometimes called Argentine barbecue sauce, it is uncooked and very easy to prepare. As an added bonus, you can use it three ways: as a marinade before cooking, as a baste during cooking, and as a condiment for serving. (Better make plenty.)

1. Using a food processor or blender, combine all of the ingredients and pulse several times until finely chopped.

2. The chimichurri sauce will keep in an airtight container in the refrigerator for up to 5 days.

Pair It   This chimichurri is equally excellent with lamb and beef. It goes especially well with the Oak-Smoke Tri-Tip (page 98).

CHIPOTLE BUTTER

Makes 1½ cups

PREP TIME: 10 MINUTES
COOK TIME: 5 MINUTES

1 cup (2 sticks) salted butter
2 chipotle chiles in adobo sauce, finely chopped
2 teaspoons adobo sauce
2 teaspoons salt
Juice of 1 lime

With artwork, you need the glue just as much as the glitter. This chipotle butter is like the glitter that makes barbecue staples such as corn on the cob and steaks pop with flavor. Insert cold slivers of the butter under the skin of chicken, add a cold pat to your resting steak, or generously slather on hot Mexican Street Corn (page 149).

1. On the stovetop, in a small saucepan over medium heat, melt the butter. Stir in the chopped chiles, adobo sauce, salt, and lime juice, continuing to stir until the salt is dissolved, about 5 minutes. Remove from the heat.

2. Serve the chipotle butter hot or cold. It will keep in an airtight container in the refrigerator for up to 2 weeks.

Technique Tip The next time you're at the hardware store, stock up on a few of those small, wooden, natural (not plastic) bristle paint brushes. They're super cheap and perfectly suited for applying a wide layer of butter to corn on the cob.

CILANTRO-BALSAMIC DRIZZLE

Makes 2 cups

PREP TIME: 5 MINUTES

½ cup balsamic vinegar

½ cup dry white wine

¼ cup extra-virgin olive oil

½ cup chopped fresh cilantro

2 teaspoons garlic powder

1 teaspoon salt

1 teaspoon freshly ground
black pepper

1 teaspoon red pepper flakes

Splash of Sriracha

This rich and fresh drizzle is a perfect topping for any roasted vegetable.

1. In a medium bowl, whisk together the balsamic vinegar, wine, olive oil, cilantro, garlic powder, salt, pepper, and red pepper flakes until well combined.

2. Add a dash of Sriracha and stir.

3. Store in an airtight container in the refrigerator for up to 2 weeks.

Pair It   Drizzle this on Brussels Sprout Bites (page 155).

SWEET POTATO MUSTARD

Makes 1½ cups

STEEPING TIME: 1 HOUR
PREP TIME: 25 MINUTES
COOK TIME: 20 MINUTES

½ cup apple cider vinegar

⅓ cup yellow mustard seeds

1 bay leaf

1 cup water

1 tablespoon molasses

1 tablespoon bourbon

⅔ cup sweet potato purée

¼ cup packed brown sugar

2 tablespoons ground mustard

½ teaspoon smoked paprika

1 teaspoon salt

½ teaspoon ground cinnamon

½ teaspoon ground allspice

½ teaspoon cayenne pepper

I am fortunate to live close to one of America's coolest hot dog joints. Jack's Cosmic Dogs, an Alton Brown favorite, is just down the road from me, in Mount Pleasant, South Carolina. The eclectic diner atmosphere is one of a kind, and the hot dogs are made even more noteworthy with a unique sweet potato mustard. You can now order Jack's mustard online, but here's my attempt at a homemade version.

1. On the stovetop, in a saucepan over medium-high heat, bring the apple cider vinegar to a boil.

2. Remove from the heat, stir in the mustard seeds and bay leaf, and let steep, uncovered, for 1 hour. Discard the bay leaf after steeping.

3. Pour the liquid into a food processor or blender, making sure to scrape in the mustard seeds as well. Add the water, molasses, and bourbon, and pulse until smooth.

4. Pour the mixture back into the saucepan over medium heat and stir in the sweet potato purée. Bring to a boil, then reduce the heat to low and cook, stirring occasionally, for 5 minutes.

5. Whisk in the brown sugar, ground mustard, smoked paprika, salt, cinnamon, allspice, and cayenne, and simmer until thickened, about 10 minutes.

6. Remove from the heat and let cool completely before refrigerating.

7. The sweet potato mustard is best served cold. It will keep in an airtight container in the refrigerator for up to 2 weeks.

Pair It Try this sweet and tart specialty mustard as a veggie dip, on hot dogs, and hamburgers, or on the Bunny Dogs with Sweet and Spicy Jalapeño Relish (page 154).

MANDARIN GLAZE

Makes 2 cups

PREP TIME: 5 MINUTES

1 (11-ounce) can mandarin oranges, with their juices

½ cup ketchup

3 tablespoons brown sugar

1 tablespoon apple cider vinegar

1 tablespoon yellow mustard

1 teaspoon ground cloves

1 teaspoon ground cinnamon

1 teaspoon garlic powder

1 teaspoon onion powder

1 teaspoon salt

1 teaspoon freshly ground black pepper

Sometimes you just gotta have something sweet. Since the 1800s, mandarin oranges have been viewed by many as a beacon of the start of the holiday season and placed in Christmas stockings as a symbolic gift. This mandarin-based sauce gets most of its sweetness from the juice of the canned version of those stout little tangerines.

1. Using a food processor or blender, combine the mandarin oranges and juice, the ketchup, brown sugar, apple cider vinegar, mustard, cloves, cinnamon, garlic powder, onion powder, salt, and pepper, and pulse until the oranges are in tiny pieces.

2. Transfer the mixture to a small saucepan on the stovetop and bring to a boil over medium heat, stirring occasionally.

3. Reduce the heat to low and simmer for 15 minutes.

4. Remove from the heat and strain out the orange pieces if desired. Serve the glaze hot.

5. The glaze will keep in an airtight container in the refrigerator for up to 5 days.

Pair It This citrus-based sauce is a hit for most pork and poultry dishes, including Savory-Sweet Turkey Legs (page 52).

JAMAICAN JERK PASTE

Makes ³/₄ *cup*

PREP TIME: 10 MINUTES

¼ cup cane syrup

8 whole cloves

6 Scotch bonnet or habanero chiles, stemmed and seeded

¼ cup chopped scallions

2 tablespoons whole allspice (pimento) berries

2 tablespoons salt

2 teaspoons freshly ground black pepper

2 teaspoons ground cinnamon

1 teaspoon cayenne pepper

1 teaspoon dried thyme

1 teaspoon ground cumin

The flavor of Jamaican Jerk comes from three main ingredients: allspice, pepper, and pimento wood smoke. You won't be able to find pimento wood pellets anywhere, but because allspice is actually made from dried pimento berries, the flavor is well represented in this recipe. Scotch bonnet chiles provide the fruity heat in this potent paste. Use it as a marinade on Jamaican Jerk Chicken Quarters (page 53).

1. In a blender or food processor, combine the cane syrup, cloves, chiles, scallions, allspice, salt, pepper, cinnamon, cayenne pepper, thyme, and cumin until smooth and sticky.

2. The paste will keep in an airtight container in the refrigerator for up to 1 week.

Pair It Use this paste on the Jamaican Jerk Chicken Quarters (page 53).

OUR HOUSE DRY RUB

Makes ¾ cup

PREP TIME: 10 MINUTES

¼ cup paprika

¼ cup turbinado sugar

3 tablespoons Cajun seasoning

1 tablespoon packed
brown sugar

1½ teaspoons chili powder

1½ teaspoons cayenne pepper

1½ teaspoons ground cumin

This is a super all-purpose barbecue rub. There's no extra salt added beyond what is in the Cajun seasoning, but trust me, it's got a lot of punch. Warning: I'm a chile head—that is, someone who *loves* spicy food—so you may want to adjust the cayenne accordingly.

1. In a small bowl, combine the paprika, turbinado sugar, Cajun seasoning, brown sugar, chili powder, cayenne pepper, and cumin.

2. Store the rub in an airtight container at room temperature for up to a month.

Pair It **I use this rub on everything. Try it on the Party Pulled Pork Shoulder (page 72).**

BLUEBERRY BBQ SAUCE

Makes 1 cup

PREP TIME: 5 MINUTES
COOK TIME: 10 MINUTES

2 cups water

½ cup minced fresh blueberries

1 tablespoon balsamic vinegar

½ cup ketchup

1 tablespoon
Worcestershire sauce

1 teaspoon Sriracha

1 teaspoon liquid smoke

1 teaspoon Dijon mustard

Salt

Freshly ground black pepper

Feeling blue? One taste of this blue-tinted sauce will perk you up and get you buzzing about how good barbecue sauce can be without a tomato base. On the Fourth of July, I'll pair this with a red sauce and the White Barbecue Sauce recipe in my free *Sides & Sauces* cookbook (see Resources, page 196), for a red, white, and blue barbecue.

1. On the stovetop, in a saucepan over low heat, simmer the water, blueberries, and balsamic vinegar for 5 minutes.

2. Stir in the ketchup, Worcestershire sauce, Sriracha, liquid smoke, and Dijon mustard, season with salt and pepper, and continue simmering for 5 minutes.

3. Remove from the heat and strain out most of the blueberry pulp.

4. The barbecue sauce will keep in an airtight container in the refrigerator for up to 1 week.

Ingredient Tip   If fresh blueberries are not available, look for high-quality frozen wild blueberries. You can even use dried blueberries!

SWEET AND SPICY JALAPEÑO RELISH

Makes 1 cup

PREP TIME: 10 MINUTES

6 jalapeño peppers, stemmed, seeded, and cut into pieces

1 serrano chile, stemmed, seeded, and cut into pieces

1 red bell pepper, stemmed, seeded, and cut into pieces

1 cucumber, coarsely chopped

1 onion, coarsely chopped

½ cup rice wine vinegar

¼ cup apple cider vinegar

2 tablespoons sugar

3 teaspoons minced garlic

1 teaspoon salt

Jalapeños have just the right amount of heat to keep you alert, but not so much that they're unbearable. The other thing that's great about jalapeños is their shelf life. Keep them refrigerated at 45°F, and they'll stay fresh for 5 or 6 weeks. Always keep some on hand to chop up this fiery relish that will add a little heat to everything from hot dogs to pork chops.

1. Using a food processor or blender, combine the jalapeños, serrano chile, bell pepper, cucumber, and onion, and pulse until coarsely chopped.

2. Add the rice wine vinegar, apple cider vinegar, sugar, minced garlic, and salt, and pulse until minced but not puréed.

3. The relish will keep in airtight container in the refrigerator for up to 1 week.

Pair It Spoon this relish on the Pickled-Pepper Pork Chops (page 78).

MEASUREMENT CONVERSIONS

Volume Equivalents (LIQUID)

US STANDARD	US STANDARD (OUNCES)	METRIC (APPROXIMATE)
2 tablespoons	1 fl. oz.	30 mL
¼ cup	2 fl. oz.	60 mL
½ cup	4 fl. oz.	120 mL
1 cup	8 fl. oz.	240 mL
1½ cups	12 fl. oz.	355 mL
2 cups or 1 pint	16 fl. oz.	475 mL
4 cups or 1 quart	32 fl. oz.	1 L
1 gallon	128 fl. oz.	4 L

Oven Temperatures

FAHRENHEIT (F)	CELSIUS (C) (APPROXIMATE)
250°	120°
300°	150°
325°	165°
350°	180°
375°	190°
400°	200°
425°	220°
450°	230°

Volume Equivalents (DRY)

US STANDARD	METRIC (APPROXIMATE)
⅛ teaspoon	0.5 mL
¼ teaspoon	1 mL
½ teaspoon	2 mL
¾ teaspoon	4 mL
1 teaspoon	5 mL
1 tablespoon	15 mL
¼ cup	59 mL
⅓ cup	79 mL
½ cup	118 mL
⅔ cup	156 mL
¾ cup	177 mL
1 cup	235 mL
2 cups or 1 pint	475 mL
3 cups	700 mL
4 cups or 1 quart	1 L

Weight Equivalents

US STANDARD	METRIC (APPROXIMATE)
½ ounce	15 g
1 ounce	30 g
2 ounces	60 g
4 ounces	115 g
8 ounces	225 g
12 ounces	340 g
16 ounces or 1 pound	455 g

RESOURCES

WEBSITES

TRAEGER

TraegerGrills.com

Head to the home of the original pellet grill manufacturer for information on new smoker models as well as FAQs and troubleshooting videos.

CAMP CHEF

CampChef.com/how-to

Camp Chef is known for a wide variety of grill types. On its extensive website, the company offers details on cooking and "how to" help.

GREEN MOUNTAIN GRILLS

GreenMountainGrills.com

Green Mountain Grills, or GMG, specializes in high-quality pellet cookers. The "Watch & Learn" area of the website offers exceptional recipes and entertaining videos.

PIT BOSS GRILLS

PitBoss-Grills.com

Pit Boss Grills are some of the most widely available pellet smokers. The company also sells a competition blend hardwood pellet mix. At the time of this writing, the Competition Blend is the most affordable wood pellet per pound, thanks to retailers like Walmart and Lowe's.

REC TEC GRILLS

RecTecGrills.com/content /Manual_OnlineVersion_021814.pdf

Rec Tec offers PDF versions of its manuals on each smoker model's product page (like the one I link to above).

PELLET HEADS FORUM

PelletHeads.com

The Pellet Heads site offers a vast library of knowledge primarily focused on the ins and outs of wood pellet grills, but it also features an active community of smokers.

BARBECUE TRICKS

BarbecueTricks.com/sauces-sides-recipes

Many of the sauce selection and cooking tips in this book were first tested at the website I founded earlier this century. You can download my personal barbecue sauce and side dish recipes free at the link above.

BALLISTIC BBQ

YouTube.com/user/sd4547

Greg Mrvich of Ballistic BBQ makes some elaborate recipes on a variety of grills. Pellet fans will want to look at his videos featuring a Yoder or Rec Tec pellet smoker.

GRATETV

GrateTV.com

Many of the slow-smoke techniques discussed in this book were originally revealed in various episodes of my online video series. Along with my friend Jack Waiboer, I shared weekly adventures in live-fire cooking and barbecue.

CAROLINA PIT MASTERS

CarolinaPitMasters.com

Jack Waiboer offers the quintessential classes on barbecuing, from patio to competition pit master. The competition course is a smart way to get on the fast track of competitive barbecue.

SERIOUS EATS

SeriousEats.com/2015/08/how-to-pick -shrimp-varieties-freshness-guide.html

The Serious Eats website is the world's most trusted authority on deliciousness. Their guide to shrimp is especially informative.

USDA WILD GAME INFORMATION

TinyURL.com/y8efjtka

The United States Department of Agriculture offers free material on safe food preparation. Here, they offer detailed tips and information on wild game purchasing and preparation from farm to table.

EWG'S DIRTY DOZEN™

EWG.org/foodnews/dirty-dozen.php

This detailed site coined the term Dirty Dozen to refer to specific produce that needs extra care in cleaning due to pesticides and other toxins. This is a great reference for investigating the merits of particular organic fruits and vegetables.

NEW HAMPSHIRE LIQUOR AND WINE OUTLETS BLOG

LiquorAndWineOutlets.com/learn_and _entertain/wine_and_food_pairings

This liquor and wine seller offers a lot of recipe and food-pairing information on its blog.

SNAKE RIVER FARMS

SnakeRiverFarms.com/preparation-guides

Snake River Farms is one of the few sources of Wagyu brisket. The website also offers detailed cooking guides with specialty beef and pork information.

BOOKS

Mrvich, Greg. ***Sous Vide BBQ: Delicious Recipes and Precision Techniques that Guarantee Smoky, Fall-Off-the-Bone BBQ Every Time.*** New York: Ulysses Press, 2018.

Greg is the founder of the Ballistic BBQ YouTube channel and has compiled a great book on using sous vide to hack the process. Greg uses pellet grills to finish the magic. Lots of smoker science is revealed.

Raichlen, Steven. ***Project Smoke: Seven Steps to Smoked Food Nirvana.*** New York: Workman Publishing, 2016.

There is now a third season of Raichlen's show based on this book. Lots of smoker testing in both the show and the book.

West, Bill. ***BBQ Blueprint: Top Tricks, Recipes, and Secret Ingredients to Help Make You Champion of the Grill.*** Charleston, SC: Triehouse Publishing, 2016.

I thought up many of the recipes and techniques in this book while I was writing my first book, ***BBQ Blueprint***, which is available from Amazon.com.

West, Bill. ***The Complete Electric Smoker Cookbook: Over 100 Tasty Recipes and Step-by-Step Techniques to Smoke Just About Everything.*** Berkeley, CA: Rockridge Press, 2017.

This was my first book for Rockridge Press, and it has gone on to become a best seller for outdoor cooking. Many of the recipes in the book can be made equally as well on a low-and-slow wood pellet grill.

RECIPE INDEX

INDEX

ABOUT THE AUTHOR

BILL WEST is a country music authority, barbecue enthusiast, and best-selling cookbook author based in Charleston, South Carolina. He's been the on-air host and operations manager of some of Charleston's leading radio stations, and has interviewed some of entertainment's biggest celebrities, including Taylor Swift, Darius Rucker, Paula Deen, Zac Brown, Ryan Seacrest, Brad Paisley, Garth Brooks, Keith Urban, Carrie Underwood, and Alton Brown, to name a few. His blog at BarbecueTricks.com and his YouTube channel have accumulated more than 8 million views and nearly 40,000 subscribers.

A native of Glenview, Illinois, West is the youngest of six children and has spent the last 30 years in the Southeast playing country music on the radio. As a hobby, he competed in and judged barbecue competitions across the state for several years before he took up writing. Armed with a degree in broadcast journalism from Bradley University in Peoria, Illinois, he took his first "real job" in sunny Hilton Head Island, South Carolina, in 1989 (just one week before Hurricane Hugo). He and his wife, MJ, make their home in Charleston and have one guitar-playing son, Jack, who is on track to become the next Jerry Reed or Chet Atkins.

Download Bill's free *Sides & Sauces* eBook:

BarbecueTricks.com/sauces-sides-recipes

Get his book *BBQ Blueprint* here:

BarbecueTricks.com/the-bbq-blueprint

Get his book *The Complete Electric Smoker Cookbook* here:

BarbecueTricks.com/electric-smoker-cookbook

Follow Bill West:

twitter.com/BarbecueTricks

facebook.com/BarbecueTricks

CPSIA information can be obtained
at www.ICGtesting.com
Printed in the USA
BVHW061442050520
578956BV00004B/9